Mental Maths
for ages 9 to 11

Teacher's book

Anita Straker

CAMBRIDGE
UNIVERSITY PRESS

For my friends Carole and Sarah,
who think numbers are fun.

PUBLISHED BY THE PRESS SYNDICATE OF THE UNIVERSITY OF CAMBRIDGE
The Pitt Building, Trumpington Street, Cambridge CB2 1RP, United Kingdom

CAMBRIDGE UNIVERSITY PRESS
The Edinburgh Building, Cambridge CB2 2RU, United Kingdom
40 West 20th Street, New York, NY10011-4211, USA
10 Stamford Road, Oakleigh, Melbourne 3166, Australia

© Cambridge University Press 1994

First published 1994
Fifth printing 1999

Printed in the United Kingdom at the University Press, Cambridge

A catalogue record for this title is available from the British Library.

ISBN 0 521 48510 X

Introduction

This series is intended to help children think about numbers and carry out mental calculations. There are three teacher's books and seven booklets of short exercises for pupils: one teacher's book and one booklet for children aged 5 to 7, a second teacher's book and two more booklets for ages 7 to 9, and a third teacher's book and three more booklets for ages 9 to 11. The final pupil's booklet is mainly for lower secondary pupils.

Mental Maths for ages 9 to 11 is the third teacher's book. It contains ideas for you to work on with groups of children or a whole class and photocopiable pages of puzzles and games for children to do by themselves. *Mental Maths 3, Mental Maths 4 and Mental Maths 5* are published separately and are intended for nine- to eleven-year-olds to work from directly, either at school or at home.

Part 1: Ways of working   Page 2

Part 1 of this book contains brief advice on things like classroom organisation and ways in which children can record their answers. It stresses the importance of counting activities and the value of discussing children's methods.

Part 2: Oral work   Page 7

Part 2 has a series of suggestions for oral work at national curriculum levels 3 to 5. Each activity is designed to be led by a teacher or classroom helper and will last for up to 10 minutes. The level of difficulty and the number skills required are indicated for each one. Many of the activities are suitable for a whole class to work on together, since questions and responses are possible at more than one level. Others are more suitable for a small group working at roughly the same level.

Part 3: Puzzles and games   Page 29

Part 3 consists of photocopiable pages of puzzles or games for children to work on by themselves. The puzzles are for individual children to do, either in school or at home. The games are intended for two or more children to play together. Most children will be able to read the instructions or the rules for themselves though less confident readers may need some help. In most cases, children will be able to complete the activity in about 15 minutes. Levels of difficulty for each activity, and solutions to the puzzles, are given on pages 60 to 62.

Part 4: Answers for *Mental Maths 3 & 4*   Page 63

Mental Maths 3, the first of the pupil's booklets for ages 9 to 11, contains exercises at levels 3 or 4 of the national curriculum; *Mental Maths 4* focuses on level 4 and touches on level 5; *Mental Maths 5* is mainly at level 5. The intention is that pupils work regularly on just one or two of the 5- to 10-minute exercises or problems each week. Answers to questions in *Mental Maths 3* and 4 are given at the back of this book on pages 63 to 70. The *Answer Book* which accompanies the whole series has answers to *Mental Maths 5*.

Part 1: Ways of working

Mental work with numbers

The importance of mental arithmetic and the ability to think about numbers in one's head is undeniable. Although many jobs require an ability to calculate using tools like calculators or computers, in everyday life an ability to deal mentally with numbers – combined with the occasional use of the back of an envelope – is of more use.

Quick recall of number facts, and confidence with mental calculations – both those where an accurate answer is required and those where an approximation is good enough – will develop only if children have frequent and varied opportunities to practise. Short sessions of five to ten minutes on most days are preferable to half-an-hour once a week. These can be fitted at the start or end of a lesson, or between two other activities, or at any time when the context provides an opportunity to talk about numbers. You could also use your sessions of thinking about numbers to:

❐ revise last week's number work;
❐ ask questions related to classroom displays;
❐ help children to use and apply mathematics to investigate or solve problems;
❐ extend their mathematical vocabulary;
❐ assess the skills of individual children.

Organising the class

To achieve an appropriate atmosphere for thinking you will need to establish how you want to work with the children. For example, you might say:

❐ Today we are going to think about numbers. We won't be using pencil and paper or calculators to help work things out - we will just use our heads.
❐ If you have something to say, or are ready to tell me your answer, don't call out as it might distract others who are still thinking.
❐ Try not to interrupt when anyone else is speaking.
❐ When you are thinking, it sometimes helps to shut your eyes.

When you are arranging groups of children to work together, it is worth considering the role that each could play. Any pupil is more likely to learn if she or he takes an active part but some individuals may dominate and others may try to withdraw from the interaction. Your role is to ask questions, observe and give feedback, directing suitable questions to particular children and encouraging the reluctant.

If a group is to be left to work on its own for a while, you may need to allocate particular responsibilities to different children. Some roles they can play are:

❏ a starter: who makes sure that everyone understands what is to be done and who calls you if the group gets stuck;

❏ an organiser: who collects whatever materials are needed for the activity, gives them out to everyone in the group, and gathers them together at the end;

❏ a reader: who helps anyone understand any difficult words;

❏ a time-keeper: who starts and stops the clock for any timed activities;

❏ a referee: who makes sure that turns are taken fairly and that everyone has an equal chance to contribute;

❏ a recorder: who has pencil and paper to note any scores;

❏ a reporter: who agrees with the group what will be reported to you or to the whole class at the end of the activity.

Recording answers in oral work

Many of the answers to your questions will be given orally. This helps to build children's confidence and speed without the need for any formal recording.

However, with larger groups or whole classes it is more difficult to involve everyone if all answers are spoken. There are various strategies for recording which give each child a chance to respond during mental arithmetic sessions. The usual way with older pupil is for them to list their answers on paper, perhaps in a small notebook kept for the purpose. Other ways which work well with smaller groups are these.

❏ For short questions with answers in the range 0 to 20, they can colour their answers on a number strip. Start each question by saying something like 'Colour this number blue.' At the end of your questions you can check responses by asking 'Which number did you colour blue?' They can compare their patterns of colours to identify any errors.

❏ For answers in the range 1 to 100, provide each of them with a 100-square. As questions are asked, numbers corresponding to answers can be covered with a counter or coloured on the square. It is easy for you to walk round the class and see who has covered what.

❏ Another way is to give each member of the group a pack of number cards. Children simply pick from their packs the card which corresponds to their answer and put it in front of them on the table top or hold it up to show you.

❏ With two-digit answers, you can use sets of double width cards for numerals 10 to 90, and single width for 1 to 9. When you ask a question, each of them places the appropriate units card on top of the tens card, and holds it on the table top while you check their responses. This also helps to reinforce place value.

$$\boxed{3 \quad 0} \quad \text{with} \quad \boxed{5} \quad \text{gives} \quad \boxed{3 \quad 5}$$

Building children's confidence

Pupils need to feel that mental maths is well within their compass. It's important to choose activities and frame questions at levels which allow them to succeed and which they can readily get to grips with. The interest and pleasure you express as you work with the class will also play a part in building their confidence.

Praise too is important, so how do you avoid discouragement when they give 'wrong' answers? Rather than saying 'yes' or 'no', you can try saying:

❐ What do other people think?
❐ Has anyone got a different answer?
❐ Are there any other possibilities?

or

❐ How did you work that out?
❐ Can you think of a way of checking that?
❐ Did anyone do it a different way?

It may be easier for children to come up with acceptable answers if you occasionally build in a longer thinking time. You could also ask them to agree an answer with a partner before going 'public'. More open-ended questions allow a wider range of possible answers and help to encourage the more diffident. For example:

❐ The answer is £15. What was the question?
❐ Can you estimate the number of words on this page, or how many postage stamps would cover this piece of paper, or how much that water tank holds …? How did you make your estimate?
❐ If you know that 20×4 is 80, what else do you know?
   (For example, $10 \times 4 = 40$, $20 \times 2 = 40$, $20 \times 0.4 = 8$, $200 \times 4 = 800$, $20 \times 40 = 800$ …)
❐ Approximately, what is $138 + 521$? What about 39×7?

Helping children to remember

Methods of mental arithmetic are based on a sound understanding of place value together with quick and accurate recall of addition and multiplication facts. Your first aim is to build up children's speed and confidence in the recall of number facts, and to extend their awareness of the number system, without worrying about formal recording. Some pupils are helped if you discuss with them what it is they need to remember; others respond well to an agreed target such as 'by the end of next week I shall know my seven times table up to 5×7'.

Repetition of multiplication tables also has its place but a mere recitation of 'Two twos are four, three twos are six …' may send them to sleep! Set the words to music, start at the end of the table and work backwards, start in the middle and go on from there, jump about from one multiple to another or make up and say a division table.

Discussing the methods used

Next you need to help children develop their own strategies for mental calculations. Few people use the standard written methods when they are working in their heads. For example, it is not uncommon in mental calculations to add the hundreds or the tens first and then the units, or the pounds before the pence. You need to point this out and draw attention to the different ways of doing things. There is no 'proper' method – children can choose whatever method suits them best.

Every so often, you should ask pupils to explain their thinking to you and their class-mates. You could also explain to them your own ways of doing things, if these are different. The purpose of this is to help them to remember and refine the strategies they are using.

You could use questions like these to help them think about their methods.

- ❑ That's interesting. Could you tell us how you did it?
- ❑ I'm not sure I understand. Could you tell us more about that?
- ❑ Could you explain why you did it that way?
- ❑ Could you check that answer by doing a different calculation?

The importance of counting

The ability to count with confidence in all kinds of situations underpins a lot of simple mental arithmetic. Almost any day can start with a quick counting activity. It is certainly worth checking at the start of the school year which of the class are confident with these lower level counting activities.

Level 2
- ❑ Count the even numbers. Count the odd numbers. Now count them backwards.
- ❑ Count in twos, starting with 16. Now start with 15. Will we get to 48? How do you know?
- ❑ Count in tens to 100, and then back to nought.
- ❑ Now start at 5 and count in tens. Will you say 73? How do you know?
- ❑ I shall say a number between 100 and 200. I want you to count on (or back) from there until I say stop.

Level 3
- ❑ Look at these cards with spots on (no more than 20, randomly arranged, but in identifiable groups such as threes, fours or fives). Can you say how many spots there are without counting one by one? How did you know?
- ❑ Estimate how many spots there are on these cards when I hold them up briefly. Who thinks there are more than 50? Can you explain why?
- ❑ How many children in the class? How many legs, arms, eyes, fingers, toes …?
- ❑ Count in twenties to 200. Now count backwards in twenties to zero.
- ❑ Count in hundreds to 1000 and back again.

- ❐ What number is the third before 31? What number is the fourth after 48?
- ❐ What number is 30 after 6? What number is 20 before 89?
- ❐ Count in threes to 30. Count in fours to 24.
- ❐ Start at 2 and count in threes. Start at 5 and count in fours.
- ❐ Start at 30 and count backwards in threes. Now start at 31.
- ❐ Start at 40 and count backwards in fours. Now start at 42.
- ❐ If we counted round the circle in fives, starting with Mary with 20, who would say 60? Think in your heads and tell me who it would be.
- ❐ If everyone wore a cardigan with 5 buttons, how many buttons would there be altogether? How did you work it out?

Level 4

- ❐ Count up to 100 in sixes, sevens, eights, nines. Now count back again.
- ❐ Count up to 100 and back again in elevens, twelves, fifteens.
- ❐ Count in twenty-fives to 1000 and back again.
  What is 75 more than 350? 50 less than 625?
- ❐ Count these chime bar sounds to yourself, then tell me how many you heard – they will be in small groups at irregular intervals.
  What strategies did you use to count?
- ❐ Take turns to count on seven and then eight. Who will be the first person to say a number more than 100? How do you know?
- ❐ Play *Fizz Buzz* by counting round the class. For any multiple of 7 say *Fizz*. For any multiple of 6 say *Buzz*. If the number has both properties, say *Fizz Buzz*.
- ❐ Count on in sixes. What number should we stop at if, when we count back in sevens, we return to the same starting number? Can you explain why?
  Are there any other possibilities?
- ❐ This pattern of beads has three red, four blue, three red, four blue …
  What colour is the 25th bead? What position is the 20th red bead?
- ❐ Count all the spots on this 6-sided dice. Is there a quick way of doing it?
  What about a dice with ten sides?
- ❐ How many words do you think there are on this page?
  What is a good way to estimate?

More hints

You will find more activities and advice about asking questions, prompting answers, developing vocabulary, and so on, in *Talking Points*, by Anita Straker, published by Cambridge University Press (ISBN 0 521 44758 5).

Part 2: Oral work

These activities are intended to be led by you or by a classroom assistant. Some are suitable for the whole class and others for small groups. Most will take about ten minutes but some will need a little longer. In many of the activities no writing is required, though pupils could record their answers in the ways described on page 3; in others, it is helpful to tabulate some of the results in order to look for patterns. An oral activity could be followed up by the group working by themselves on a game or puzzle which draws on the same range of skills.

1 Elevenses

Objectives
Level 3:
addition and subtraction facts to 20.

Organisation
Work with a group of four or five children.

Words to stress
Add, plus, subtract, minus, difference; more, fewer; sum, total, altogether, equals.

Preparation
Take a pack of playing cards. Remove the jacks, queens and kings.

Procedure
Game 1
Shuffle the cards and spread them face down on the table. Children take turns to turn over two cards. If the sum is 11, the two cards are kept. If not, they are replaced face down on the table. Continue until all the cards are won. Children who are familiar with this game can carry on playing by themselves.

Game 2
Shuffle the cards. Put out the first nine cards face up in three rows of three. Children take turns to look for pairs of cards which total 11. These cards are then covered with the next two cards from the pack. Continue until there are no combinations to cover or all the cards are used. As a variation, look for trios which total 11.

In both games, some questions to ask are:

❑ What is the sum of your two numbers?
❑ Are there fewer spades or fewer clubs?
❑ What is the difference between 11 and your total?

② Staircases

Objectives
Level 3:
addition facts to 20.

Organisation
Work with a group of any size.

Words to stress
Add, plus, sum, total, altogether, equals; twice, double.

Preparation
You need a board or wall-chart on which to keep a record.

Procedure
Introduce this investigation by drawing a staircase with 5 steps. Tell the children that they can climb the stairs either one step at a time or two at a time. Ask:

❑ In how many different ways can you climb the stairs? *(Eight different ways: 1, 1, 1, 1, 1 or 1, 1, 1, 2 or 1, 1, 2, 1 or 1, 2, 1, 1 or 2, 1, 1, 1 or 1, 2, 2 or 2, 1, 2 or 2, 2, 1)*
❑ What if you tried 6 steps, or 1, 2, 3, 4 steps?
❑ Is there a pattern? *(1, 2, 3, 5, 8, 13 … Each number is the sum of the previous two)*
❑ Can you predict the number of ways for 7 steps? *(21)* Check and see if you were right.

---

③ Oddities

Objectives
Level 3:
addition facts to 20;
odd and even numbers.

Organisation
Work with a group of any size.

Words to stress
Add, plus, sum, total, altogether, equals; odd, even, pair.

Preparation
You need a board or wall-chart on which to keep a record.

Procedure
Tell the children they can use the same odd number more than once in this investigation. Ask:

❑ What pairs of odd numbers will add to make 10? *(1,9 or 3,7 or 5,5)* What pairs of odd numbers will add to make 20? *(1,19 or 3,17 or 5,15 or 7,13 or 9,11)*
❑ How many ways are there in which three odd numbers have a total of 10? Can you explain your answer? *(None, since the sum of two odd numbers is even, the sum of three odd numbers is odd and so cannot equal 10)*
❑ What are the ways of adding four odd numbers to make 10? Can you explain how you worked it out? *(Each pair must have an even sum, and be derived from 2,8 or 4,6, giving 1,1,1,7 or 1,1,3,5 or 1,3,3,3)*
❑ Which four odd numbers will add to make 20? *(1,1,1,17 or 1,1,3,15 or 1,1,5,13 or 1,1,7,11 or 1,1,9,9 or 1,3,3,13 or 1,3,5,11 or 1,3,7,9 or 1,5,5,9 or 1,5,7,7 or 3,3,3,11 or 3,3,5,9 or 3,3,7,7 or 3,5,5,7 or 5,5,5,5)*

Summit

Objectives
Level 3:
addition or subtraction of a single digit to or from a two-digit number.

Organisation
Work with a group of any size, or the whole class. Smaller groups can work on easier or more difficult sets of numbers.

Words to stress
Add, plus, sum, total, altogether, equals.

Preparation
You need a board or wall-chart on which to keep a record.

Procedure
Introduce the investigation to the children with the numbers 1, 2 and 3. Ask them to consider the different totals that could be made if each digit was put in one of these boxes.

Three different totals can be made: 15 (as 12 + 3 or 13 + 2), 24 (as 21 + 3 or 23 + 1) and 33 (as 31 + 2 or 32 + 1). If subtraction rather than addition is used, the possible differences that can be made are 9, 11, 18, 22, 29 and 31.

Now choose four digits, such as 3, 5, 6 and 8. What are the different totals that can be made by selecting three of the digits to fill the boxes? There are 12 altogether to find. Suitable questions to ask are:

❑ What three digits will you pick?
❑ What is the sum of your two numbers?
  How did you work that out?
❑ Can you make a different total with those digits?
❑ How shall we record this? Is there a systematic way?
❑ What is the largest sum you can make? Explain why.
  What is the smallest sum you can make? Why?
❑ What if digits could be repeated? What new totals could you make now?

On another day, extend the investigation to finding differences.

❑ What differences could we make from three of these four digits? (Up to 24, depending on the digits. With 3, 5, 6 and 8, there are 23, since 63 − 8 equals 58 − 3.)
❑ What is the biggest difference you can make? Why?
  What is the smallest difference you can make? Why?
❑ Can you find four digits that produce 24 distinct differences?

⑤ Polygon patterns

Objectives
Levels 3, 4:
repeated addition and
multiples of 3, 4, 5, 6.

Organisation
Work with a group of
any size.

Words to stress
Add, sum, total,
altogether, pattern,
multiple, table,
odd, even.

Preparation
You need some straws with which to form shapes. With a
larger group you could draw on a board instead.

Procedure
Introduce the investigation.

One △ needs three straws.

Two △▷ needs how many straws?

Three △▷△ needs how many straws?

❑ How many straws for five triangles? For eight?
❑ How many triangles if 13 straws are used? *(6)*
❑ Is there a systematic way to record it? *For example,*

No. of triangles	1	2	3	4	5	6	7
No. of straws	3	5	7	9	11	13	15

❑ Is there a pattern? Can you continue it? Why does it
go up in twos?
❑ How many straws are needed to make 10 triangles?
(21) How did you work it out?
❑ What do the numbers of straws have in common?
❑ What if we tried squares? How many straws are
needed for ten squares? *(31)* What is the pattern now?
Why does the pattern go up in threes?
❑ How many squares would there be if you used 30
straws? *(9 with two straws left)* Can you predict how
many straws for a given number of squares? *(3n + 1)*
❑ What if we tried hexagons? *(5n + 1)*
❑ What happens if you try pentagons? *(40 straws form a
ring of 10 pentagons. Only 3 straws are needed for the last.)*

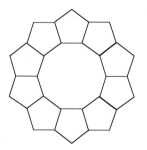

6 Fold and cut

Objectives
Levels 3, 4:
odd and even numbers;
two times table,
four times table.

Organisation
Work with a small group.

Words to stress
halve, double;
odd, even.

Preparation
You need some paper strips and pairs of scissors, and pencil and paper for recording.

Procedure

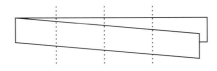 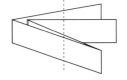

One fold, three cuts   Two folds, one cut

Take a strip of paper and fold it in half. Cut once across the middle. Before unfolding and separating ask:

❏ How many separate pieces do you think there are. *(3)*
❏ What if I make more than one cut?
❏ How should we record what we are doing?
   (Tabulate the number of cuts and the number of pieces)
❏ Is there a pattern? *(3, 5, 7, 9 ... Each number is two more than the previous number; all the numbers are odd)*
❏ Is there a relationship between the number of cuts and the number of pieces? *(The number of pieces is one more than double the number of cuts)*
❏ What if I fold twice before cutting?
   (The pattern is 5, 9, 13, 17 ..., or one more than four times the number of cuts)

7 Twos

Objectives
Levels 3, 4:
addition facts to 20;
multiplication and division by 1, 2, 3 or 4;
addition and subtraction of two-digit numbers.

Organisation
Work with a group of any size, or the whole class.

Preparation
You need a board or wall-chart on which to keep a record.

Procedure
Use three 2s with any signs (+, −, × or ÷) to make as many different numbers as possible. For example:

$$2 \times 2 \times 2 = 8$$
$$22 \div 2 = 11$$
$$2 + (2 \div 2) = 3$$
$$2 + 2^2 = 6$$

Words to stress
Add, plus, sum, total,
altogether, equals;
product, multiply,
divide;
twice, double, halve.

❏ What other numbers can you make with three 2s?
❏ What numbers can you make with four 2s?
❏ Can you make 50 with seven 2s? *(For example,*
22 + 22 + 2 + 2 + 2 or (22 × 2) + 2 × ((2 ÷ 2) + 2).)
❏ What numbers can you make with 3s?
❏ Can you make all the numbers from 1 to 40 with the
digits 1, 2, 3, 4? For example:

1	2×3–4–1	11	12+3–4	21	2×4+13	31	43–12
2	1+2+3–4	12	2×4+3+1	22	34–12	32	12×3–4
3	2×3+1–4	13	12+4–3	23	4×3×2–1	33	132÷4
4	1+2+4–3	14	21–3–4	24	4×3×2×1	34	(14+3)×2
5	12–3–4	15	13+4–2	25	4×3×2+1	35	32+4–1
6	1+3+4–2	16	(34÷2)–1	26	24+3–1	36	4×1+32
7	31–24	17	1×34÷2	27	32–4–1	37	24+13
8	2+3+4–1	18	32–14	28	23+4+1	38	42–3–1
9	23–14	19	13+4+2	29	42–13	39	4×2+31
10	1+2+3+4	20	21+3–4	30	13×2+4	40	12×3+4

⑧ Bracelets

Objectives
Levels 3, 4:
addition facts to 20;
multiplication and
division facts to 10 × 10.

Organisation
Work with a group of
any size, or the whole
class. Smaller groups
can be formed to
investigate different
pairs of numbers with
results collected later.

Words to stress
Add, plus, sum, total,
altogether, equals;
multiply, remainder.

Preparation
You need a board or wall-chart on which to keep a record.

Procedure
Choose any two single-digit numbers. Make a number
chain by using this rule: add the previous two numbers
and write down the units digit. This is what happens with
8 and 4.

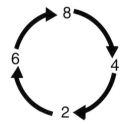

Investigate other pairs of starting numbers. Suitable
questions to ask are:

❏ How many different bracelets are there? *(Five)*
❏ What is the shortest? *(5, 5, 0)*
❏ How many links in the longest? *(60)*
❏ What if you multiply instead of adding? *(Six bracelets,*
disregarding 1, 1, 1 … 5, 5, 5 … and 6, 6, 6 …)
What if you write the remainder after dividing by 7,
instead of 10? *(Three bracelets with 3, 8 and 24 links)*

9 Count up

Objectives
Levels 3, 4:
addition of a single digit to a two-digit number.

Organisation
Work with a group of any size.

Words to stress
Add, sum, total, altogether.

Preparation
None.

Procedure
Choose two numbers less than 10. Counting round the group, add each number in turn and say the new total. For example, if 7 and 8 are chosen the totals would go:

7, 15, 22, 30, 37, 45, 52, 60, 67, 75, 82, 90, 97, 105.

The game stops when someone makes the total 100 or more. That person is then out of the game. Ask:

❐ Did you notice any patterns?
How would the pattern continue after 100?
❐ What is the sequence of every second number?
How does this relate to the two chosen numbers?
❐ Stop when you get to 80 or more. Can you predict who will reach 100 or more? Can you say why?

10 Addition patterns

Objectives
Level 4:
addition of two-digit numbers.

Organisation
Work with a group of any size. Pairs of children can investigate different sets of numbers with results collected later.

Words to stress
Add, plus, sum, total.

Preparation
You need a board or wall-chart for demonstrating. The children need plain paper and a pencil.

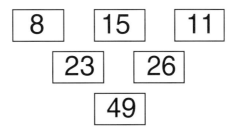

Procedure
Show the children a pattern like the one above and ask them to say how it works. *(Start by choosing any three different numbers less than 20. For the next row, add pairs of numbers that are next to each other.)* The children should investigate different addition patterns using three different numbers to start with each time. Then ask:

❐ How many different arrangements are there of the same three starting numbers? *(6)*

❐ Is the final number always the same? *(Three different final numbers are produced by the six arrangements)*
❐ Which arrangement gives the smallest final number? *(The smallest number in the centre to start with)*
❐ Which arrangement gives the biggest final number? *(The largest number in the centre to start with)*
❐ Can you predict the final number? *(Sum of the three numbers plus the one in the centre)*
❐ What happens with four numbers to start with?

 ## Subtraction patterns

Objectives
Level 4:
subtraction of two-digit numbers.

Organisation
Work with a group of any size. Pairs of children can investigate different sets of numbers with results collected later.

Words to stress
Minus, subtract, difference.

Preparation
You need a board or wall-chart for demonstrating. The children need plain paper and a pencil.

Procedure
Show the children a subtraction pattern.

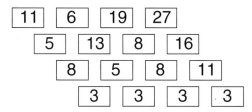

Ask the children to explain how this pattern works. *(Start by choosing any four numbers less than 30. For the next row, find the differences between numbers next to each other; the last number in the row is the difference between the first and fourth numbers in the row above.)* Then ask:

❐ What happens with different starting numbers?
❐ Do bigger numbers produce more rows?
(Not necessarily)
❐ Which numbers produce most rows? *(At most ten rows are produced by numbers up to 30 e.g. by (0,2,6,13) and its complementary set (13,11,7,0), which has the same set of differences, or by (0,3,9,19) and (19,16,10,0).
By adding the same number to each number in the set, further sets can be found, since (1,3,7,14), (2,4,8,15), and so on, all result in the same second row as (0,2,6,13).
Up to 31, eleven rows are generated, by (0,5,14,31) and (31,26,17,0). Up to 100, thirteen rows can be generated: for example, by (0,35,54,64) or by (0,52,80,95).)*
❐ Is there a relationship between the numbers in the second row? *(Sometimes two pairs add to the same total; sometimes the biggest number is the sum of the others.)*

(12) Chains

Objectives
Level 4:
multiplication and
division by 2 and 3.

Organisation
Work with a group of
any size, or the whole
class. Pairs of children
can investigate different
starting numbers.

Words to stress
Mutiply, divide;
halve, treble.

Preparation
None.

Procedure
Choose a starting number less than 30. Make a number
chain by using these rules: if the number is even, halve it;
if the number is odd, mutiply by 3 and add 1.

$$6 \ -3 \ -10 \ -5 \ -16 \ -8 \ -4 \ -2 \ -1$$

Investigate other starting numbers up to 30. Ask:

❑ What is the longest chain you can find?
   (27 produces a chain with 112 numbers)
❑ Can you record your results on one diagram? *(For
   example, 24 results in the same chain as 6 after two steps)*
❑ What happens with numbers greater than 30?
   (97 produces a chain with 119 numbers)
❑ What if the second rule is multiply by 3 and subtract 1?
   (It sometimes ends in a loop: for example, 20, 10, 5, 14, 7)

---

(13) Relations

Objectives
Level 4:
two-digit numbers and
the four rules.

Organisation
Work with a group of
any size.

Words to stress
Add, plus, subtract,
minus, multiply, divide,
product, factor.

Preparation
You need a board or wall-chart to write a list of numbers.

Procedure
In turn, each child in the group suggests a one- or two-
digit number. Write these on the board in a horizontal
line, but randomly positioned. For example:

14, 36, 9, 63, 15, 17 ...

Children then take turns to make up a 'story' relating
successive pairs. Remind them that each one will involve
a third number. Encourage them to make their 'stories'
interesting, and different from others. For example:

If you add 22 to 14 you get 36.
36 divided by 4 is 9.
9 lollies at 7p each cost 63p.
3 is a common factor of 63 and 15.
15 girls and 17 boys in a class total 32 children.

(14) Lu-lu

Objectives
Level 4:
addition of a three single digit numbers;
addition of 2 two-digit numbers.

Organisation
Work with a small group.

Words to stress
Sum, total, add, plus, altogether, equals.

Preparation
You need three dice and pencil and paper to keep scores.

Procedure
This game is based on one played in Hawaii. Players take turns to throw all three dice. Only fours, fives or sixes count towards a player's score. The first to reach 100 (or any other total) wins the game. It helps to nominate one of the group to keep a record of the scores, but each player should add mentally the fours, fives or sixes thrown, and then add mentally the sum to their previous total. Suitable questions to ask during the game are:

❏ Which dice count? What is their total?
❏ How could you score 16? *(4, 6, 6 or 5, 5, 6)*
❏ What scores are possible after one throw?
 (All numbers from 4 to 18, with the exception of 7)
❏ Could you score 30 in exactly three throws? How?
 (By scoring 10 three times, or 9, 10 and 11, or ...)
❏ When you added 17 to 36, how did you work it out?

An extra rule, once players know the game, is this. Any dice showing 1, 2 or 3 is rethrown for a bonus by the next player, who adds any 4, 5 or 6 to their own total.

(15) Differences

Objectives
Level 4:
subtraction of two two-digit numbers.

Preparation
None.

Procedure
Start working with the whole group. Take any two digits other than zero. Make the greatest and least numbers possible with them – for example, 6 and 3 give 63 and 36. Find the difference between these two numbers. Use the answer as your next two digits and repeat the process.

63 – 36 ➡ 72 – 27 ➡ 54 – 45 ➡ 9

Organisation

Work with a group of any size, or the whole class. Once children know what to do, small groups can investigate different pairs of digits.

Words to stress

Minus, subtract, fewer, less, difference.

Suitable questions to ask during the investigation are:

❏ Which two digits will you choose?
  What is the value of the tens digit?
❏ What is the smallest number you can make with your two digits? Why? What is the largest number? Why?
❏ What is the difference between your numbers?
  How many fewer is ... than ...?
  Subtract ... from ... What do you get?
❏ What happens? *(You always get to 9)*
❏ How many subtractions do you need to do before you reach the end of the chain?
❏ Which pairs of numbers need the greatest number of subtractions? *(31, 42, 53, 64, 75, 86, 97, representing the larger number formed from the pair of digits, need five)*
❏ Is there a pattern? *(Numbers in this sequence differ by 11; the sums of their two digits are 4, 6, 8, 10 ... 16.)*
❏ What happens if you allow zero? *(90 and 20 need five)*

 # Split it up

Objectives

Level 4:
addition of a series of single digits; multiplication and division facts to 10×10.

Organisation

Work with a group of any size, or the whole class.

Words to stress

Add, plus, sum, total, altogether, equals; multiply, product, divisible by, factor.

Preparation

You need a board or wall-chart to keep a record.

Procedure

Split up the number 12. Multiply the parts together.

$12 = 9 + 3$	$9 \times 3 = 27$
$12 = 7 + 3 + 2$	$7 \times 3 \times 2 = 42$
$12 = 6 + 3 + 2 + 1$	$6 \times 3 \times 2 \times 1 = 36$

Suitable questions to ask are:

❏ Can you make a product of 32? *(8 × 4)*
  Are there any other possibilities? *(8 × 2 × 2)*
❏ Can you make a product of 40?
  (5 × 4 × 2 × 1 or 5 × 2 × 2 × 2 × 1)
  What about 44? *(This isn't possible as 11 would need to be a factor, leaving 1 as the other factor)*
❏ What is the largest product you can make?
  (81, made from 3 × 3 × 3 × 3)
❏ What if you split up 10?
  (Maximum is 36, made from 4 × 3 × 3)
❏ What if you split up 14?
  (Maximum is 162, made from 2 × 3 × 3 × 3 × 3)

More splits

Objectives
Level 4:
addition of two-digit numbers;
multiplication and division by 7 or 11.

Organisation
Work with a small group.

Words to stress
Sum, total, difference; product, factor, multiple, divisor.

Preparation
None.

Procedure
Ask the children to split up 50 into two numbers, one divisible by 11 and the other divisible by 7. *(22 and 28)* Let them try on their own for a while, then ask:

☐ Is there a systematic way to do this?
(For example, list the multiple of 7 and the multiples of 11 up to 50, then look at the possible totals of different pairs)
☐ Can you do the same thing for 100? *((4 × 11) + (8 × 7))*
☐ How did you tackle it?
(A quick way is to double the result for 50)
☐ Can you predict the result for 150? Check your prediction to see if it works out. *((6 × 11) + (12 × 7))*
☐ What would you predict for 75? *((3 × 11) + (6 × 7))*

18 **Adders**

Objectives
Level 4:
addition of two-digit numbers;
multiplication facts to 10 × 10.

Organisation
Work with a small group.

Words to stress
Sum, total;
average, mean.

Preparation
None.

Procedure
Ask the children to work out this sum.

$$1 + 2 + 3 + 4 + 5 + \ldots + 20$$

Then ask:

☐ How many different ways of doing this can you find?
(Split into groups of 4, 5 or 10 numbers and find sub-totals. For example, find the sum of 1 to 5; the sum of 6 to 10 is then 5 × 5 plus the sum of 1 to 5, and so on.
Or pair off numbers with an easily added total such as 12 or 20; mark off these pairs and see what is left.
Or pair off numbers from either end to get 10 totals of 21.)
☐ What is the average (mean) of the first 20 whole numbers? *(210 ÷ 20 or 10.5)* How did you work it out?
☐ Can you use one of your ways to find the sum and average of the first 50 whole numbers? *(1275, 25.5)* The first 100 whole numbers? *(5050, 50.5)*
☐ Is there a general rule for working out the sum of the first n whole numbers? *(Half of $n \times (n + 1)$)*

(19) Noah's animals

Objectives
Level 4:
division by 2, 3 or 5.

Organisation
Work with a small group.

Words to stress
Divisible by, multiple of; odd, even, factor.

Preparation
None.

Procedure
Tell the children they are to work out how many animals Noah squeezed into his Ark. When the animals paired off in twos, one was left over. When they grouped in threes, one was left over. But when the animals grouped in fives, not one was left over. After a while, ask:

❏ How many animals were there if one remained after they grouped in twos? *(Any odd number)*
❏ How many animals were there if they could grouped in fives with none left?
   (A multiple of five: that is, a number ending in 5 or 0)
❏ Are numbers ending in zero odd or even?
❏ How many animals were there if one remained after they grouped in threes? *(4, 7, 10, 13, 16, 19, 22, 25 …)*
❏ Which number fits all the conditions? *(25)*
❏ 25 is one possibility. Are there others? *(55, 85, 105 …)*
❏ Is there a pattern? *(The next number is 30 more)*
❏ What is the relationship between 30, and the ways that the animals grouped? *(30 = 2 × 3 × 5)*
❏ How many animals were there if they grouped in:
   fours and one remained;
   sevens and five remained;
   nines and seven remained? *(61)*

Rectangles

Objectives
Level 4:
calculation of the area and perimeter of a rectangle;
addition of single-digit numbers;
multiplication facts.

Organisation
Work with a group of any size.

Words to stress
Area, perimeter;
half, double;
sum, product.

Preparation
You need six straws, with two cut in half, to make eight altogether: four of 2 units in length and four of 4 units.

Procedure
Show the children that it is possible to make rectangles from the straws by demonstrating one example.

Ask the children to imagine some different rectangles that could be made from the straws. Use the straws only to demonstrate any impossibilities. Encourage them to think about the numbers by asking questions like these.

❐ What do you know about the opposite sides of a rectangle? How many of the straws do you need to make one long side and one short side? *(Half of them)*
❐ Imagine a rectangle? How long is it? How wide is it?
❐ What is its perimeter? What is its area?
❐ Could you make another rectangle with a longer (shorter) perimeter? With a bigger (smaller) area? Is there a sytematic way of recording this?
❐ How many different perimeters are there? Which is the longest?
❐ How many different areas? Which is the largest?
❐ Do rectangles of the same area have equal perimeters? Do those with the same perimeter have equal areas?

Possible rectangles	Width	Length	Area	Perimeter
2 × 2	2	2	4	8
2 × 4	2	4	8	12
2 × (2 + 4)	2	6	12	16
2 × (4 + 4)	2	8	16	20
2 × (2 + 4 + 4)	2	10	20	24
4 × 4	4	4	16	16
4 × (2 + 2)	4	4	16	16
4 × (2 + 4)	4	6	24	20
4 × (2 + 2 + 4)	4	8	32	24
(2 + 2) × (4 + 4)	4	8	32	24
(2 + 4) × (2 + 4)	6	6	36	24

(21) Pick up

Objectives
Level 4:
subtraction of a series of single-digit numbers; multiples of 10.

Organisation
Work with a group of up to six children.

Words to stress
Sum, total, difference, add, subtract; multiple, factor.

Preparation
You need a set of cocktails sticks or other small objects that can be picked up easily.

Procedure
Put 30 sticks in a pile in the centre of the table. Tell the children that they are to play a game taking turns to pick up from the pile any number of sticks from 1 to 9. The one who picks up the last stick in the pile wins the game.

Children are likely to play randomly at first. After a while, discuss with them what happens when particular numbers of sticks are left in the pile.

❒ How many sticks will you take? How many does that leave in the pile?
❒ How shall we record each move?
❒ What happens if there are 10 sticks left in the pile? Who should win? *(The next but one player)* Why? *(Whatever number of sticks is taken by the next player, the following player will be able to pick up all the sticks left)*
❒ What happens if there are 20 sticks left? Who should win then?
❒ What if just two people play the game? Who can always win? *(The second player)*
❒ What if we start with 60 sticks in the pile? What are the winning numbers of sticks? *(50, 40, 30, 20, 10)* What is the same about all these numbers? *(They are all multiples of 10)*
❒ Who will win if we start with 35 sticks? Why?
❒ What if we started with 22 sticks, and you could only pick up 1, 2, 3 or 4 sticks? Who should win? *(The first player)*
❒ What are the winning numbers of sticks? *(20, 15, 10, 5)* What is the same about all these numbers? *(They are all multiples of 5, which is one more than the number of sticks that can be picked up)*

(22) Sports shop

Objectives
Level 4:
addition and subtraction of two-digit numbers; approximation of a total.

Organisation
Work with a group of any size, or the whole class.

Words to stress
Price, cost, amount, sum, total, more, difference; estimate, approximate, round.

Preparation
Paste some pictures of different sports items on card. Label them with prices up to £50. On another day, use a different selection of objects and prices.

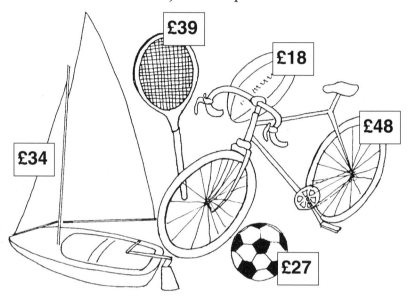

Procedure
Put questions to individuals, as appropriate.

❑ What does the ... cost to the nearest £10?
❑ Approximately, what would you pay for the ... and the ...? What is the exact cost?
❑ What about the ..., the ... and the ...?
❑ What is the approximate difference in price between the ... and the ...? The exact difference?
❑ How much more than the ... is the ...?
❑ What change is there from £50 if we buy the ...?
❑ What change will we get from £100 if we buy the ... and the ...?
❑ What two things could you buy for less than £70?
   (£18, £18 or £18, £27 or £18, £34 or £18, £48 or £27, £27 or £27, £34 or £27, £39 or £34, £34)
   How much change from £70 would you get?
   (£34, £25, £18, £4, £16, £9, £4, £2)
❑ Could you buy three things for exactly £100?
   (£18, £34, £48 or £27, £34, £39)
❑ How many 50p coins would you pay for the ...?
❑ What would ten of the ... cost?
❑ What would one hundred cost?
❑ What is one-tenth of the price of the ...?

Eating out

Preparation

Get the children to prepare and illustrate some menus with a range of priced items. The prices should be chosen to suit the attainment levels of the children in the group.

Ye olde Tea Shoppe	
Pot of tea	60p
Toast	25p
Bun	25p
Scone	30p
Cream	35p
Jam	20p
Muffin	40p

Fritz Fast Food	
Burger	85p
Fries	45p
Pizza	65p
Chicken	75p
Coke	25p
Coffee	40p

Procedure

Provide two sheets of paper for each menu. Each should be headed with the name of the café. On one sheet children should make up questions to ask about their menu. Answers to their questions should be written on the second sheet. You may need to give some guidance in the types of questions that might be asked, such as:

❐ A family of four bought two pots of tea, two buns and two scones at the Tea Shoppe.
How much did it all cost?
❐ What is the cost of eight buns? Of seven scones?
❐ Which is more expensive: a scone with cream and jam or two muffins?

❐ What is the total cost of all the food on Fritz's menu?
❐ What is the difference in price between two pizzas and three portions of fries?
❐ Dan and Rhia bought a burger, some fries and two cokes. They shared the cost between them. How much did each of them pay?

Groups can then exchange their menus and questions for others to work out the answers. These can be returned to the original group for marking or the answer sheets can be passed on.

How many dinosaurs?

Objectives
Levels 4, 5:
estimation of a number of objects less than 100.

Organisation
Work with the whole class.

Words to stress
Estimate, total, average, mean, mode, range, frequency, data.

Preparation
You need a clear plastic jar of fewer than 100 dinosaurs or other small toys; a grid labelled 10, 20, 30 ... across the bottom drawn on a board or wall chart; a one hundred square (the kind produced commercially on which cubes can be stacked is ideal, but a home-made square on which counters can be placed will do); a counter or cube for each pupil and some coloured pens.

Procedure
Children should take turns to hold the jar, shake it, and look at it from different angles, in order to estimate the number of objects in the jar. Each child records their estimate by putting a cube or counter on the 100-square. If two or more make the same guess, they stack their cubes on the appropriate number. Questions to ask are:

❑ What is the range of the estimates?
❑ Which is the most common estimate (the mode)?
❑ What's the likely average of the estimates (the mean)?
❑ What do you think the likely number of dinosaurs is now that you have seen everyone's guess?

Next, each child should record their estimate on the bar graph by placing a cross in the appropriate column. For a guess of 68 a cross would be placed between 60 and 70; a guess of 70 would go in the same column but a guess of 60 would go between 50 and 60.

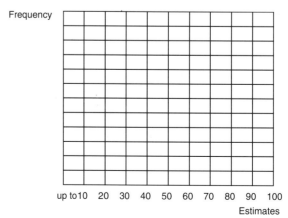

Suitable questions to ask now are:

❒ What do you think the likely number of dinosaurs is now that you have seen the graph?
❒ What is the range of the estimates?
❒ Which gives a better idea of the likely number of dinosaurs, the 100-square or the bar chart? Why?
❒ Which gives the range of estimates more accurately?

Finally, give out handfuls of the objects to be counted. Write each one's total on the board and ask the class to find the grand total. Check the count by doing this again but varying the size of the handfuls. Ask:

❒ How many guesses were within 10 of the right total?
❒ What was the difference between your guess and the correct total, Lisa?
❒ Can you estimate how many dinosaurs there would be in a jar twice the size? Three times the size?

25 Big ideas

Objectives
Level 5:
estimates using single-digit powers of 10 and multiplication facts to 10 × 10.

Organisation
Work with two teams.

Words to stress
Roughly, estimate, approximately; multiply, product, factor.

Preparation
You need coloured pens or chalk and a calculator. Write out two sets of four numbers and draw a blank 4 × 4 grid. Fill the grid randomly with the 16 possible products of a number from Set A with one from Set B. This is what one grid might look like when prepared.

840	342	468	680
624	408	703	630
306	760	1295	962
456	1400	629	1040

Set A: {17, 35, 26, 19}   Set B: {24, 37, 18, 40}

Procedure
Two teams take turns to try to make one of the numbers on the grid by estimating the product of any number in Set A and any number in Set B. If correct (check with the calculator) the number is coloured. The winner is the first team to get three numbers in a straight line. Ask:

❒ Which number can you make? How did you estimate? What information did you use?

(26) Bigger and smaller

Objectives
Level 5:
estimates using powers
of 10.

Organisation
Work with the whole
class, directing easier
questions to some and
more difficult questions
to others.

Words to stress
Roughly, approximately,
estimate;
tenth, hundredth,
decimal place.

Preparation
You need an empty litre jug and a board or wall-chart to
record a table.

Procedure
Hold up a litre jug. Ask the children to name something
about 1 litre in capacity. Make a note of it. Now ask them
to name things which hold about 10 litres. Build a table
similar to the one below. Emphasise that as you go up or
down the list, you are multiplying or dividing by 10.

100 000 litre	the school swimming pool
10 000 litre	a milk tanker
1 000 litre	a domestic oil tank
100 litre	a bath
10 litre	a bucket
1 litre	a bottle of lemonade
0.1 litre	a coffee cup
0.01 litre	a matchbox
0.001 litre	a tiny thimble
0.0001 litre	a single drop of water

Now ask the children questions like these:

❐ What is approximately ten times the capacity of a
matchbox?
❐ What is one hundredth the capacity of a coffee cup?
❐ How many buckets of water would fill the swimming
pool?
❐ How many thimbles could be filled from the water in
a bath?
❐ What is equivalent to a million drops of water?

Similar activities can be carried out making estimates of
length (or distance), area or weight. Children generally
find it easiest to suggest estimates of length or of area.
Capacity (or volume) and weight are harder to visualise.

(27) Feed the world

Objectives
Level 5:
addition of powers of 10, 2 or 3.

Organisation
Work with a small group.

Words to stress
Multiply, product, factor, power, index.

Preparation
You need one dice, and pencil and paper to record scores.

Procedure
Children are to imagine that they are raising funds for charity. They take turns to roll the dice. The number rolled represents the power to which 10 must be raised, so if 5 is rolled, 10^5 or £100000 is collected. The aim for the group is to accumulate £10m. An alternative is to collect powers of 2 or 3 each time, with the group aiming to make a total of £500 or £2500 respectively. Ask:

❑ How much money did you obtain that time?
❑ How much have you collected altogether, Kate?
❑ How much has the group as a whole collected?

(28) Roller

Objectives
Level 5:
simple probability; addition of a series of single-digit numbers; addition of 2 two-digit numbers.

Organisation
Work with a group of from four to six children.

Words to stress
Sum, total, odd, even; likely, unlikely, fair, unfair, probability.

Preparation
You need two dice, and pencil and paper to keep scores.

Procedure
Children take turns to roll one of the dice as many times as they choose, accumulating their score as they do so. If the number rolled is 1, the score for that turn is lost. Otherwise the score is added to the player's previous total. The first to reach 100 (or any other total) wins.

It helps to ask one of the group to keep a record of the scores, but each player should add mentally their accumulated score, and then add that to their previous total.

Another option is to use two dice. This time a player's score is lost if a total of 7 is rolled.

Suitable questions to ask are:

❏ When you added 27 to 45, how did you work it out?
❏ How frequently does 1 occur?
❏ What is the longest run of numbers thrown before 1 is rolled?
❏ What is the best strategy to adopt? Why?

 Fair's fair

Objectives
Levels 5, 6: justification of the probability of an event.

Organisation
Work with two small teams.

Words to stress
Sum, total, odd, even; likely, unlikely, fair, unfair, probability.

Preparation
You need a set of dominoes and a bag to put them in.

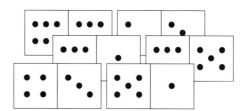

Procedure
Each team takes turns to take a domino from the bag, to say whether the total number of spots is odd or even, and put the domino back. The first team scores a point only if they pick a domino with an odd number of spots. The second team scores only if they pick a domino with an even number of spots.

Suitable questions to ask during the activity are:

❏ Is that domino odd or even? How do you know?
❏ Are the two numbers that form the sum odd or even?
❏ How shall we record the scores?
❏ Who is winning? Why? Is this a fair game?
❏ Are you more likely to pick an odd or an even domino? Why?
❏ What is the total number of dominoes? *(28)* How many of them are odd? *(12)*
❏ What is the probability of picking an odd domino? *(12/28 or 3/7)* An even domino? *(4/7)*
❏ If one team scored a point for picking a domino with six spots on one half, and the other team scored a point for picking five spots, would this be a fair game? *(Yes)* Why? *(There are seven of each kind of domino)*
❏ What is the probability of drawing a domino with three spots? *(7/28 or 1/4)*

Part 3: Puzzles and games

These number activities are intended for children to work on independently without aids like counters, pencil and paper or a calculator. Most will take from 15 to 20 minutes to complete, assuming that games are played several times. The puzzles are for individual children to work on at school or at home, and several of them can be used more than once. The games are for two or more children to play together.

The games and puzzles provide situations for children to think logically. They offer good opportunities for planning, predicting, learning from mistakes or unproductive moves, spotting a successful strategy and pursuing it, and so on. Where it is appropriate you could ask children to:

❐ consider the possible opening moves and which is the best;
❐ consider the positions possible after one, two or three moves;
❐ devise ways of recording patterns of moves;
❐ find the least number of moves needed;
❐ predict and then test who will win the game;
❐ consider whether a draw is a possibility;
❐ show that something is impossible;
❐ talk or write about winning and losing strategies;
❐ alter the rules in some way in order to see what happens;
❐ extend the puzzle or game and try to generalise it.

Besides offering ample opportunities for children to use and apply mathematics, the puzzles and games also:

❐ provide varied contexts for children to practise quick recall of number facts and mental arithmetic skills;
❐ allow you to assess their progress by observing what they do and listening to what they say.

Some of the evidence you might look for as children undertake these activities is:

❐ growing confidence as indicated by the questions children ask: for example, 'Shall I try … ?' compared with 'What shall I do now?';
❐ the speed and accuracy of their recall;
❐ their ability to talk clearly about what they have been doing, to you or to their class-mates, or to write about or record their work in some way;
❐ their ability to persevere in finding solutions;
❐ their willingness to work cooperatively with others.

The level of difficulty and the skills required in each of the puzzles and games, with solutions to the puzzles, are given in the notes on pages 60 to 62.

1 Triangles

Name:

Use each of the numbers 1, 2, 3, 4, 5 and 6.
Put one number in each circle.

1 Make each side add up to 9.

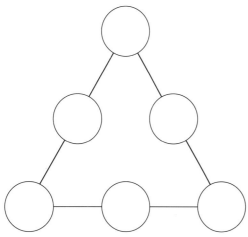

2 Make each side add up to 10.

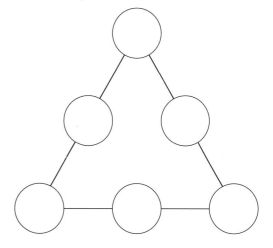

3 Make each side add up to 11.

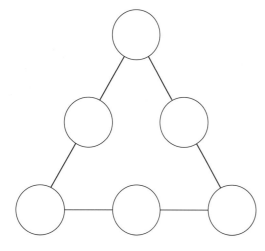

4 Make each side add up to 12.

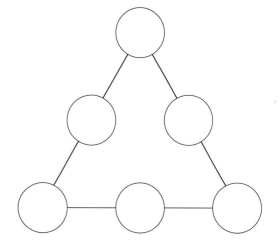

(1) (2) (3) (4) (5) (6)

From *Mental Maths* Anita Straker © Cambridge University Press 1994

Write a number in each box. You can use a number more than once but all eight numbers in each grid must total 20.

1 Each side must add up to 7.
Find different ways of doing it.

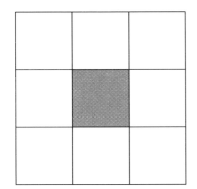 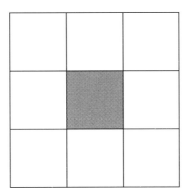 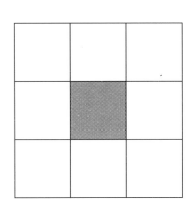

2 Now make each side add up to 8.
Find different ways of doing it.

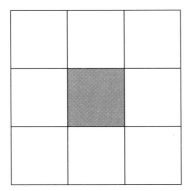 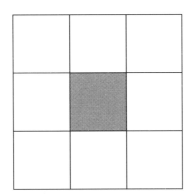 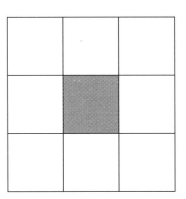

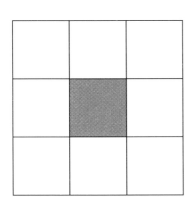 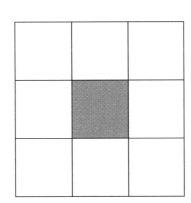 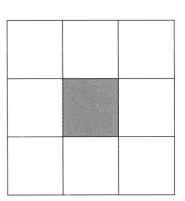

Name:

Choose a total from 15 to 20. Write it in this box.

Find three numbers that add up to your total.
Each of the three numbers must be different.

Investigate different ways of doing it.

☐ + ☐ + ☐   ☐ + ☐ + ☐   ☐ + ☐ + ☐

☐ + ☐ + ☐   ☐ + ☐ + ☐   ☐ + ☐ + ☐

☐ + ☐ + ☐   ☐ + ☐ + ☐   ☐ + ☐ + ☐

☐ + ☐ + ☐   ☐ + ☐ + ☐   ☐ + ☐ + ☐

If you can think of any more ways, use these boxes.

☐ + ☐ + ☐   ☐ + ☐ + ☐   ☐ + ☐ + ☐

☐ + ☐ + ☐   ☐ + ☐ + ☐   ☐ + ☐ + ☐

☐ + ☐ + ☐   ☐ + ☐ + ☐   ☐ + ☐ + ☐

☐ + ☐ + ☐   ☐ + ☐ + ☐   ☐ + ☐ + ☐

From *Mental Maths* Anita Straker © Cambridge University Press 1994

Name:

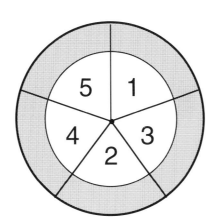

Imagine three darts on the board.
More than one dart can be on a number.
A shaded area scores double the number in the middle.

Investigate different ways of scoring 13.
Shade the box lightly if the number is a double.

☐ + ☐ + ☐   ☐ + ☐ + ☐   ☐ + ☐ + ☐

☐ + ☐ + ☐   ☐ + ☐ + ☐   ☐ + ☐ + ☐

☐ + ☐ + ☐   ☐ + ☐ + ☐   ☐ + ☐ + ☐

☐ + ☐ + ☐   ☐ + ☐ + ☐   ☐ + ☐ + ☐

☐ + ☐ + ☐   ☐ + ☐ + ☐   ☐ + ☐ + ☐

How many different ways of scoring 14 are there?   ☐
Use the back of this sheet to keep a record.

Name:

Choose a sign to put in each box.

| + | − | × | ÷ | = |

Make each sum correct.

| 10 | ☐ | 2 | ☐ | 1 | ☐ | 6 |

| 5 | ☐ | 3 | ☐ | 3 | ☐ | 12 |

| 6 | ☐ | 2 | ☐ | 3 | ☐ | 4 |

| 4 | ☐ | 10 | ☐ | 2 | ☐ | 20 |

| 6 | ☐ | 3 | ☐ | 4 | ☐ | 2 |

| 2 | ☐ | 5 | ☐ | 15 | ☐ | 8 |

| 6 | ☐ | 4 | ☐ | 9 | ☐ | 11 |

| 5 | ☐ | 8 | ☐ | 4 | ☐ | 10 |

| 1 | | 15 | | 3 | ☐ | 4 |

  From *Mental Maths* Anita Straker © Cambridge University Press 199

Name:

Imagine you have eight straws.

1 cm ———	5 cm ————————
2 cm ————	6 cm —————————
3 cm —————	7 cm ——————————
4 cm ——————	8 cm ———————————

Investigate different ways of making rectangles.
You must use all eight straws for each rectangle.

Width (cm)	Length (cm)	Width (cm)	Length (cm)	Perimeter (cm)
1 + 6	3 + 8	7	2 + 4 + 5	36

Sums

Name:

1 Use only these numbers.

(28) (45) (39) (53)

Put a number in each box to make each sum correct.

[ ] + [ ] = 98   [ ] − [ ] = 17

[ ] + [ ] = 81   [ ] − [ ] = 8

[ ] + [ ] = 84   [ ] − [ ] = 11

[ ] + [ ] = 92   [ ] − [ ] = 6

[ ] + [ ] = 73   [ ] − [ ] = 25

2 Write a number between 30 and 70 in each circle.

Use your four numbers to make up some sums.
Use a different pair of numbers each time.

[ ] + [ ] = [ ]   [ ] − [ ] = [ ]

[ ] + [ ] = [ ]   [ ] − [ ] = [ ]

[ ] + [ ] = [ ]   [ ] − [ ] = [ ]

       From *Mental Maths* Anita Straker © Cambridge University Press 1994

The pegs on each line make a pattern.
Fill in the missing numbers.

1 — | 5 | 8 | | | | 20 | | |

2 — | | 14 | | | 35 | | | |

3 — | | 48 | | | | | | 18 |

4 — | 18 | | | | | 66 | |

5 — | | | 70 | | 52 | | | |

6 — | 32 | | | | | | | 4 |

7 — | | | 49 | | 39 | | | |

8 — | 2 | | | 20 | | | | |

9 — | | 4 | | | 32 | | |

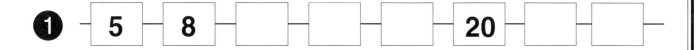

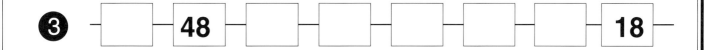

(9) Stamps

Choose two different values from 6p to 9p for stamps.

[ ] p and [ ] p.

What parcels can you send using exactly 10 of these stamps?

Stamps	Total value

From *Mental Maths* Anita Straker © Cambridge University Press 1994

1 Put 6 or 7 on each truck to make 39.

$$39 = \boxed{} + \boxed{} + \boxed{} + \boxed{} + \boxed{} + \boxed{}$$

2 Put 5 or 9 on each truck to make 38.

$$38 = \boxed{} + \boxed{} + \boxed{} + \boxed{} + \boxed{} + \boxed{}$$

3 Put 7 or 8 on each truck to make 46.

$$46 = \boxed{} + \boxed{} + \boxed{} + \boxed{} + \boxed{} + \boxed{}$$

4 Put 5 or 8 on each truck to make 45.

$$45 = \boxed{} + \boxed{} + \boxed{} + \boxed{} + \boxed{} + \boxed{}$$

5 Put 8 or 9 on each truck to make 51.

$$51 = \boxed{} + \boxed{} + \boxed{} + \boxed{} + \boxed{} + \boxed{}$$

Name:

Complete these multiplication tables.

1

×	4	7	6	3
8				
3				
5				
9				

2

×		4	9	
		8		
3				
	35			14
				2

3

×				
		24		15
	54			
	6		4	
		56		

From *Mental Maths* Anita Straker © Cambridge University Press 1994

(12) Chickens

A farmer wants to make a run for his chickens.

He has 40 metres of chain link fence to enclose a rectangular area.

What areas could he enclose?
Complete the table.

Width (m)	Length (m)	Area (m^2)
1		
2		
3		
4		
5		
6		
7		
8		
9		
10		

Which rectangle encloses the largest area?

Name:

Imagine you have 48 cubes.

Investigate ways of arranging
the 48 cubes as a cuboid.

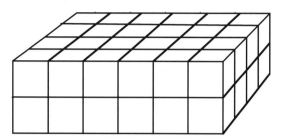

Work out the surface area
of each cuboid.

Length	Width	Height	Squares on each face						Surface area

From *Mental Maths* Anita Straker © Cambridge University Press 1994

Name:

Mrs Jones bought 15 bottles of lemonade at 28p each.

$$15 \times 28 = 420$$

so Mrs Jones paid £4.20.

Use this to work out the cost of:

16 bottles of lemonade

8 bottles of lemonade

24 bottles of lemonade

30 bottles of lemonade

45 bottles of lemonade

15 bottles at 14p each

15 bottles at 7p each

15 bottles at 8p each

15 bottles at 29p each

one tin of beans if
28 tins cost £4.20

15 Patterns

Name:

Write a multiplication fact such as 6 × 7 = 42 in the centre ring.
Write a 'sum' which you can deduce from this fact in each box.

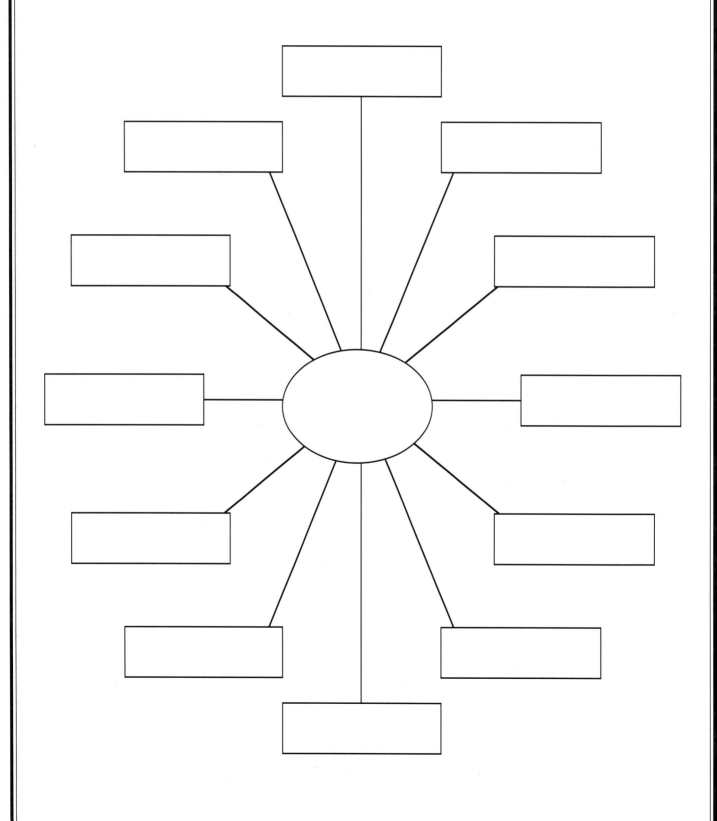

 From *Mental Maths* Anita Straker © Cambridge University Press 1994

Name:

Some numbers are equal to the sum of two squares.
For example,

$$34 = 3^2 + 5^2$$

Which numbers less than 100 are equal to the sum of two squares? Complete the table.

$+$	1^2	2^2	3^2	4^2	5^2	6^2	7^2
1^2							
2^2							
3^2							
4^2							
5^2			34				
6^2							
7^2							

Use your table. Write these as the sum of three squares.

19 = ☐ + ☐ + ☐   65 = ☐ + ☐ + ☐

41 = ☐ + ☐ + ☐   75 = ☐ + ☐ + ☐

50 = ☐ + ☐ + ☐   94 = ☐ + ☐ + ☐

Name:

Complete this puzzle. You will need to work out which numbers the letters a, b, c and d stand for.

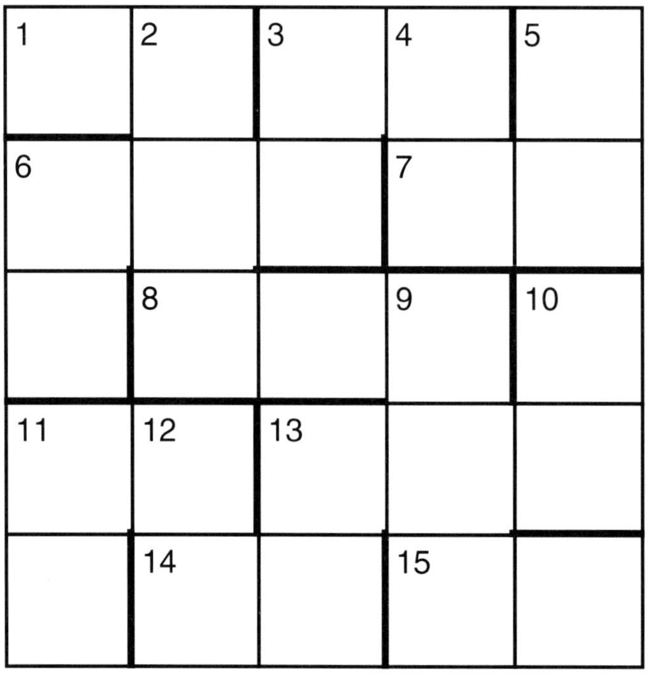

1	2	3	4	5
6			7	
	8		9	10
11	12	13		
	14		15	

Clues across

1 $3 \times a$

3 2^5

6 $14 \times d$

7 $2^2 \times 3^2$

8 $20^2 + 2^5$

11 a^2

13 $10 \times c$

14 b^2

15 $2^3 \times a$

Clues down

2 c^2

3 $3 \times d$

4 $2^4 + a$

5 $a^2 - 3$

6 2×3^2

9 $(2 \times d^2) + 5^2$

10 $5 \times b$

11 $6 \times b$

12 $10^2 - 2^2$

13 $2 \times a$

  From *Mental Maths* Anita Straker © Cambridge University Press 199

(18) Decimals

Write a decimal fraction such as 0.3 or 0.7 in this box. ☐

Make up 'sums'. Each answer must equal your decimal fraction.

1 Use at least one + sign in each of these.

☐ ☐

☐ ☐

2 Use at least one − sign in each of these.

☐ ☐

☐ ☐

3 Use at least one × sign in each of these.

☐ ☐

☐ ☐

4 Use at least one ÷ sign in each of these.

☐ ☐

☐ ☐

 **Quinze**

A game for two players

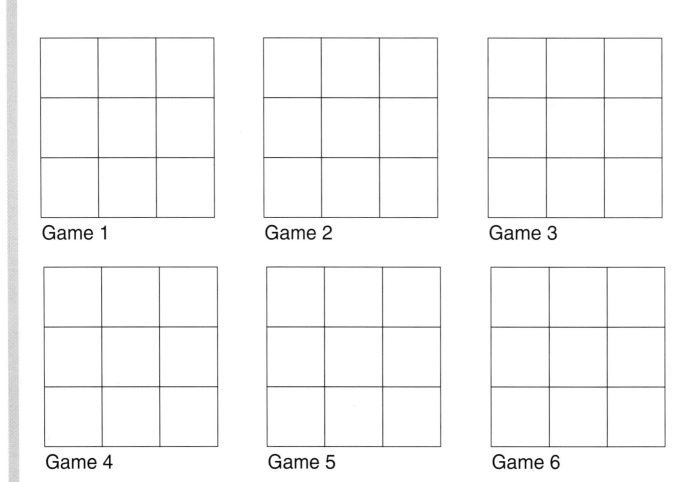

Game 1

Game 2

Game 3

Game 4

Game 5

Game 6

Rules

Take turns to go first.

The player to go first uses the odd numbers: 1, 3, 5, 7, 9.
The other player uses the even numbers: 2, 4, 6, 8.
Each number can be used only once.

Take turns to put a number on the grid.
A player who makes a line of three numbers with a sum
of 15 scores a point.

The one with most points when the grid is full wins the game.

 From *Mental Maths* Anita Straker © Cambridge University Press 19

Make 25 A game for two players

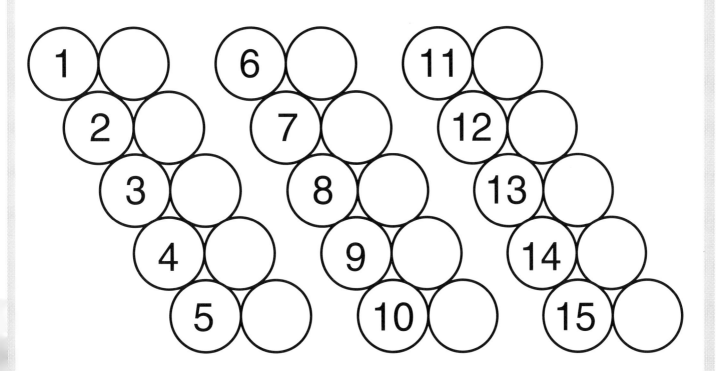

Rules

Each player needs eight small counters of their own colour.
Take turns to go first.

In turn, put a counter in a blank circle.

Only one counter can be put in each circle.

The winner is the first to get any **three** of their own
counters next to numbers that add up to 25.

You might need to place **four or more** of your counters
before three of them total 25.

Make 31　　　A game for two or three players

1	2	3	4	5	6
1	2	3	4	5	6
1	2	3	4	5	6
1	2	3	4	5	6

Rules

You need about 20 counters.

One player puts a counter on any number and says it.

Take turns to put another counter on an uncovered number. Add on that number and say the new total.

Only one counter can be put on each number.

The winner is the player to make the total exactly 31.

If you go over 31 you lose the game.

From *Mental Maths* Anita Straker © Cambridge University Press 1994

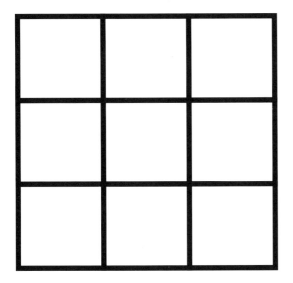 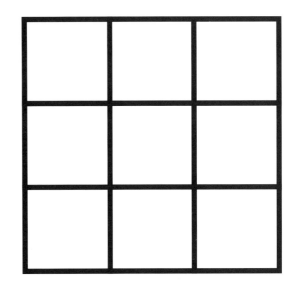

Rules

You need a pencil and two dice.

Use one grid each.

Take turns to throw both dice.
Multiply the two numbers.
Write the product in any space on your grid.
Carry on until each grid is full of numbers.

Change over grids.
Take turns to throw the dice again.
If you can, cross out the product of the two numbers.

The winner is the first to cross out all their numbers.

rom *Mental Maths* Anita Straker © Cambridge University Press 1994

Hideaway   A game for two to four players

| 1 | 2 | 3 | 4 | 5 | 6 | 7 | 8 | 9 |

Rules

You need nine small counters and two dice,
and pencil and paper to keep the score.

The first player rolls the two dice.
Use the total rolled to hide one or more of the numbers on
the board with a counter.
For example, if a total of 6 is rolled then 6 could be covered,
or 1 and 5, or 2 and 4, or 1, 2 and 3.

Only one counter may be put on a number.

The first player continues to roll the two dice until all the
numbers are hidden, or it is impossible to cover a number.
If any numbers are uncovered, the player scores penalty
points equal to their sum.

The next player then has a turn.

The winner is the one with fewest penalty points after an
agreed number of rounds.

     From *Mental Maths* Anita Straker © Cambridge University Press 1994

6 Four in a line

A game for two teams

12	41	4	38	26	11	34
9	30	36	16	2	20	39
25	1	18	40	31	27	17
15	35	29	7	21	5	33
42	22	10	3	13	28	23
6	32	14	24	37	19	8

Rules

You need three dice.
Each team needs some small counters of their own colour.

Take turns to roll the three dice.
Make a number on the board with the three numbers,
and cover it with one of your counters.

For example, with 6, 4 and 5 you could make:
$2 = (6 + 4) \div 5$, or $29 = 4 \times 6 + 5$, or $39 = 45 - 6$.

The winner is the first team to get four of their counters in a line, either horizontally, vertically or diagonally.

From *Mental Maths* Anita Straker © Cambridge University Press 1994

53

7 Countdown

A game for two to four players

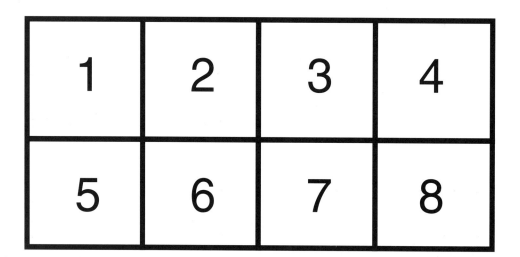

Rules

You need a counter.
Take turns to go first.

The first player places the counter on any number on the board and chooses a starting total between 50 and 100.

In turn, players push the counter to another number, subtract that number and say the new total.

The winner is the player to reduce the total to exactly zero. A player who goes below zero loses the game.

For a change, you could try to count down to –50, starting between +40 and +50.

From *Mental Maths* Anita Straker © Cambridge University Press 1994

8 Chains

A game for two to four players

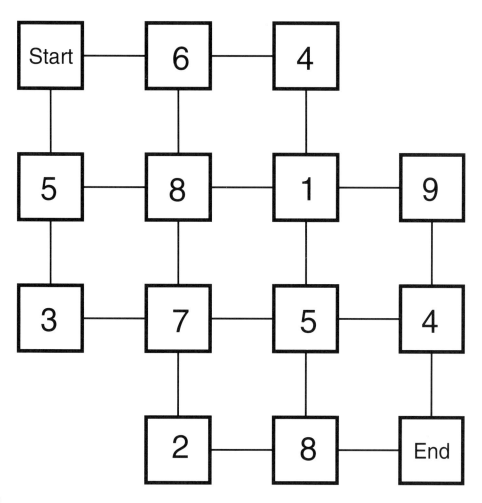

Rules

You need a counter and pencil and paper to keep the score.

The first player names a target between 20 and 80.
The other players take turns to try to make this target.

Put the counter on 'Start' and push it along the lines to 'End'.
Keep a running total of the numbers you pass through.
Your chain can pass through a number more than once.

The first player wins points equal to the difference between the target and the total of the other player's chain.

The player with most points after one round wins that game.

...m Mental Maths Anita Straker © Cambridge University Press 1994

A game for two or three players or teams

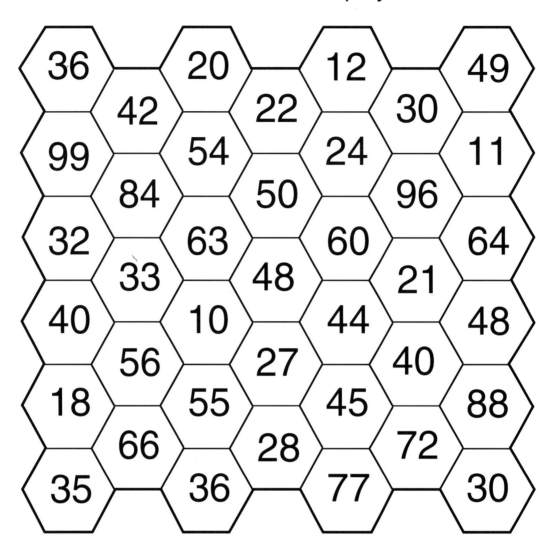

Rules

You need two dice.
Each team needs some small counters of their own colour.

Teams take turns to throw the two dice. Add the numbers.
Cover a multiple of the sum of the spots with a counter.

The winner is the first team to get four counters in a line.

For a change, aim to get a block of four counters,
or to make a chain of counters from one side to the other.

From *Mental Maths* Anita Straker © Cambridge University Press 19

(10) Fillings

A game for two players or teams

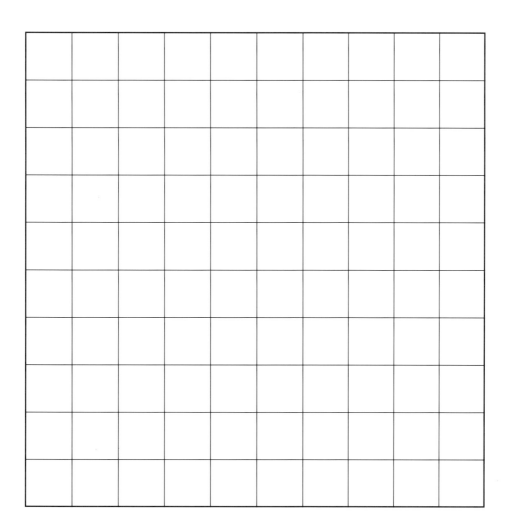

Rules

You need three dice, and a coloured pen for each team.

Teams take turns to throw the three dice. Choose any two of the numbers thrown for the length and width of a rectangle.

Colour the rectangle on the board.
Rectangles may not overlap.

Keep a running total of the area covered by your team.
The winner is the team with the largest total area coloured after six throws each.

A game for two players and a referee

4800	90	320	150	250
240	4000	400	40	300
1500	180	2400	120	480
3000	48	1800	640	3200
2000	360	200	1200	30

Rules

Each player needs some counters of their own colour.
The referee needs a calculator.

Players take turns to choose any two of these numbers.

3   5   6   8   30   40   50   60   80

Multiply them together to make a number on the board.
The referee checks with the calculator. If correct,
the player covers the number with one of their counters.

The winner is the first player to get four of their counters
in a straight line in any direction.

    From *Mental Maths* Anita Straker © Cambridge University Press 19

(12) Cross-over

A game for two players

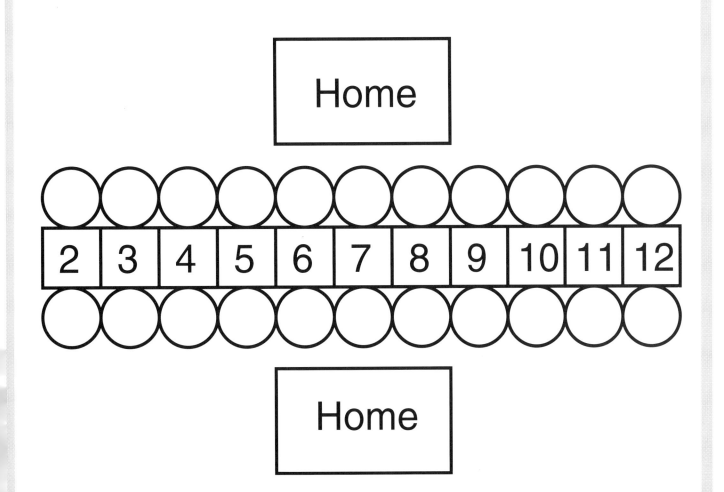

Rules

You need two dice, and 10 small counters for each player.

Each player puts their counters on the circles on one side of the road. More than one counter can be put on a circle.

Take turns to throw the two dice.
The sum of the spots shows the position from which one of your counters can cross the road to get home.

The winner is the first to get all their counters across.

Notes on the puzzles and games

Level 3

1   Triangles   Sum of three digits from 1 to 6. Subtraction from 9, 10, 11 or 12.

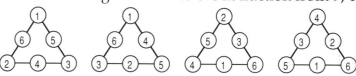

2   Line up   Addition and subtraction facts to 20.

7 in a line   6 ways

8 in a line   9 ways

3   Splits   Addition of three numbers to total from 15 to 20.

There are 12 ways of making 15:

1, 2, 12;	1, 3, 11;	1, 4, 10;	1, 5, 9;	1, 6, 8;	2, 3, 10;
2, 4, 9;	2, 5, 8;	2, 6, 7;	3, 4, 8;	3, 5, 7;	4, 5, 6.

16 in 14 ways, 17 in 16 ways, 18 in 19 ways, 19 in 21 ways, 20 in 24 ways.

4   Darts   Multiples of 2. Addition of three numbers to total 13.

For a total score of 13, there are 15 combinations:

d5, d1, 1;	d5, 2, 1;	d4, d2, 1;	d4, d1, 3;	d4, 4, 1;	d4, 3, 2;
d3, d3, 1;	d3, d2, 3;	d3, d1, 5;	d3, 4, 3;	d3, 2, 5;	d2, d2, 5;
d2, 4, 5;	5, 5, 3;	5, 4, 4.	For 14, there are 16 combinations.

5   Signs   Multiplication and division to 5×5.

For example, $10 \div 2 + 1 = 6$ $5 \times 3 - 3 = 12$ $6 \times 2 = 3 \times 4$ $4 \times 10 \div 2 = 20$

$6 = 3 \times 4 \div 2$ $2 + 5 = 15 - 8$ $6 - 4 + 9 = 11$ $5 \times 8 \div 4 = 10$ $1 = 15 \div 3 - 4$

Level 4

6   Perimeters   Sum of a series of single digits to total 18.

The sum of the digits is 36 (the perimeter) so length + width = 18.

Many solutions are possible: for example, it is possible to make

3×15, 4×14, 5×13, 6×12, 7×11, 8×10, 9×9 rectangles.

Some can be made in more than one way: for example, the four sides of the

5×13 rectangle can be either 1+4, 6+7, 5, 2+3+8 or 2+3, 6+7, 1+4, 5+8.

7   Sums   Sums and differences of pairs of two-digit numbers.

$45 + 53 = 98$	$28 + 53 = 81$	$39 + 45 = 84$	$53 + 39 = 92$	$28 + 45 = 73$
$45 - 28 = 17$	$53 - 45 = 8$	$39 - 28 = 11$	$45 - 39 = 6$	$53 - 28 = 25$

8 Pegs

Subtraction of 2 two-digit numbers.
Simple division. Addition of a single-digit number.

5, 8, 11, 14, 17 …	7, 14, 21, 28, 35 …	53, 48, 43, 38, 33 …
18, 26, 34, 42, 50 …	88, 79, 70, 61, 52 …	32, 28, 24, 20, 16 …
59, 54, 49, 44, 39 …	2, 8, 14, 20, 26 …	–3, 4, 11, 18, 25 …

9 Stamps

Multiplication by 6, 7, 8, 9. Addition of 2 two-digit numbers.
If the stamps are a and b:
$10a$, $9a+b$, $8a+2b$, $7a+3b$, $6a+4b$, $5a+5b$, $4a+6b$, $3a+7b$, $2a+8b$, $a+9b$, $10b$.

10 Trains

Multiplication facts to 10×10. Addition of two-digit numbers.
$39=3\times6+3\times7$; $38=4\times5+2\times9$; $46=2\times7+4\times8$; $45=1\times5+5\times8$; $51=3\times8+3\times9$.

11 Tables

Multiplication and division facts to 10×10.

×	4	7	6	3
8	32	56	48	24
3	12	21	18	9
5	20	35	30	15
9	36	63	54	27

×	5	4	9	2
2	10	8	18	4
3	15	12	27	6
7	35	28	63	14
1	5	4	9	2

×	6	8	4	5
3	18	24	12	15
9	54	72	36	45
1	6	8	4	5
7	42	56	28	35

12 Chickens

Multiplication of a number up to 20 by a single digit.
Areas in m^2 are: $1\times19=19$; $2\times18=36$; $3\times17=51$; $4\times16=64$;
$5\times15=75$; $6\times14=84$; $7\times13=91$; $8\times12=96$; $9\times11=99$; $10\times10=100$.
The largest area is the 10×10 square.

13 Cuboids

Multiplication facts. Addition of 6 one- or two-digit numbers.
Possible cuboids are: 1, 1, 48;   1, 2, 24;   1, 3, 16;   1, 4, 12;
1, 6, 8;   2, 2, 12;   2, 3, 8;   2, 4, 6;   3, 4, 4.
Surface areas: 194,   148,   134,   128,   124,   104,   92,   88,   80.

Level 5

14 Lemonade

Halving and doubling of sums of money.
Addition or subtraction of pence to pounds and pence.

£4.48	£2.24	£6.72	£8.40	£12.60
£2.10	£1.05	£1.20	£4.35	15p.

15 Patterns

Using patterns to calculate products and quotients.
Examples of what can be deduced from $7 \times 6 = 42$ are:

$42 \div 7 = 6$	$7 \times 12 = 84$	$14 \times 6 = 84$	$7 \times 3 = 21$
$70 \times 6 = 420$	$70 \times 60 = 4200$	$7 \times 0.6 = 4.2$	$7 \times 7 = 49$
$8 \times 6 = 48$	$3.5 \times 6 = 21$	$1.75 \times 6 = 10.5$	$1.75 \times 3 = 5.25$
one sixth of 42 = 7		two sixths (one third) of 42 = 14	
one seventh of 42 = 6		one fourteenth of 42 = 3	

16 Square sums

Index notation for square numbers.
Addition of two-digit numbers.

$19 = 1 + 9 + 9$		$65 = 4 + 25 + 36$
$41 = 9 + 16 + 16$		$75 = 25 + 25 + 25$
$= 1 + 4 + 36$		$= 1 + 25 + 49$
$50 = 9 + 16 + 25$		$94 = 9 + 36 + 49$

+	1^2	2^2	3^2	4^2	5^2	6^2	7^2
1^2	2	5	10	17	26	37	50
2^2	5	8	13	20	29	40	53
3^2	10	13	18	25	34	45	58
4^2	17	20	25	32	41	52	65
5^2	26	29	34	41	50	61	74
6^2	37	40	45	52	61	72	85
7^2	50	53	58	65	74	85	98

| 17 | Power game | Multiplication facts to 10×10.
Powers of small whole numbers.
Addition of two-digit numbers.
$a = 7 \quad b = 8 \quad c = 12 \quad d = 10$ |

1 2	2 1	3 3	4 2	5 4
6 1	4	0	7 3	6
8 8	4	3	9 2	10 4
11 4	12 9	13 1	2	0
8	14 6	4	15 5	6

| 18 | Decimals | Use of the four rules with decimal fractions. |

The games

Level 3

| 1 | Quinze | Addition of three numbers from 1 to 9 to total 15.
Use of the properties of odd and even numbers. |
| 2 | Make 25 | Addition of three numbers from 1 to 15 to total 25. |

Levels 3, 4

| 3 | Make 31 | Addition of a series of digits from 1 to 6 to total 31. |
| 4 | Roll over | Multiplication facts to 6×6. |

Level 4

5	Hideaway	Addition of several single digits with a total up to 12. Addition of two-digit numbers.
6	Four in a row	Use of the four rules, with an answer from 1 to 42.
7	Countdown	Subtraction of a series of digits from 1 to 8 to reach 0 or –50.
8	Chains	Addition of a series of digits from 1 to 9 to total from 20 to 80. Subtraction of 2 two-digit numbers.

Levels 4, 5

| 9 | Gozinto | Multiplication facts to 12×12. |
| 10 | Fillings | Addition of up to 6 one- or two-digit numbers to make a total less than 100. |

Level 5

| 11 | Whoppers | Mutiplication and division involving multiples of 10 or 100. |
| 12 | Cross-over | Sum of two numbers from 1 to 6.
Use of the probability that when two dice are rolled some totals are likely occur more frequently than others. |

Answers: *Mental maths 3*

Mental Maths 3 builds on *Mental Maths 2*. It introduces the addition and subtraction of a single digit, and of multiples of 10 or 100, to or from any two- or three-digit number. Multiplication tables for 2s to 6s and 10s are covered. Multiplication and division of up to three-digit whole numbers by 10 or 100 is introduced. Knowledge of place value up to 10000, and of tenths then hundredths as decimals, is drawn upon. Thirds, sixths and eighths are introduced, also simple areas and perimeters, the gram, millimetre and millilitre, and angles measured in multiples of 30°.

Task 1a

1 36
2 12
3 15
4 18
5 56
6 11
7 27
8 £1.25
9 60
10 18

Task 1b

1 8 right angles
2 Grams
3 1022, 1202, 2012
4 £1.20
5 Three eighths
6 £6
7 Two thousands
8 7 boxes
9 10 millimetres
10 2 metres

Task 1c

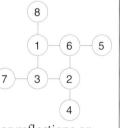

or reflections or rotations of this.

Task 1d

1 64
2 18
3 12
4 56
5 0
6 40
7 420
8 8 corners
9 16
10 13

Task 2a

1 2017
2 £1.50
3 4210
4 360°
5 80
6 2.55 p.m.
7 8 times
8 Millilitres
9 40
10 50 grams

Task 2b

1 112
2 100
3 84
4 30
5 32
6 50 coins
7 50p
8 3510
9 68
10 7

Task 2c

1 24
2 9
3 6700
4 26
5 152
6 15p
7 199
8 102
9 32
10 30 coins

Task 2d

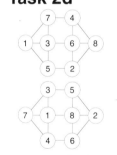

are two solutions.

Task 3a

1 35 days
2 30
3 49
4 50 millilitres
5 9, 3 and 1
6 368 cm
7 km (or miles)
8 8 right angles.
9 12 pairs
10 2.5 miles

Task 3b

Task 3c

1 5070
2 Apples
3 8 tables
4 £15.50
5 75
6 62p
7 6 faces
8 12
9 One quarter
10 4 scores

Task 3d

1 116
2 35p
3 500
4 98
5 27
6 20p
7 130
8 498
9 24
10 35

Task 4a

1 67
2 35
3 27
4 4300
5 31
6 20
7 50
8 4
9 150
10 38

Task 4b

Each line totals 23. Other arrangements are possible. With 5 or 9 in the centre, lines can be made to total 25 or 27.

Task 4c

1 86
2 32
3 9
4 33
5 8
6 40p
7 22
8 7
9 300
10 36

Task 4d

1 28
2 8 and 13
3 13 and 7
4 26
5 7, 8 and 15
6 11 and 13
7 No
8 7, 13 and 15
9 54
10 Carol:18 Mark:28

Task 5a

1 47
2 310
3 36
4 54
5 15
6 55
7 0
8 25
9 36
10 4

Task 5b

1 1:35 (25 to 2)
2 10
3 7002
4 7 teams
5 20 minutes
6 50
7 1 metre
8 5 children
9 22
10 96 miles

Task 5c

1 7
2 9
3 5
4 5
5 6
6 10
7 12
8 3
9 8
10 6

Task 5d

1 38
2 21
3 7.5 or $7\frac{1}{2}$
4 13
5 31
6 199
7 28
8 11
9 25
10 35

Task 6a

1 12 cm
2 18 and 21
3 £1,50p,10p,5p
4 A cuboid
5 0.7
6 2 left over
7 200
8 7 bags
9 1 metre
10 15 rectangles

Task 6b

1 18
2 66
3 740
4 55
5 60
6 18
7 40
8 9
9 37
10 Nearer to 70

Task 6c

1 45
2 8
3 33
4 80p
5 63
6 45
7 27
8 32
9 7
10 250

Task 6d

1 50
2 45
3 25
4 55
5 65
6 35
7 70
8 70
9 75

Task 7a

1 94
2 18
3 20
4 39
5 47
6 34
7 74
8 10
9 16
10 8

Task 7b

1 13p
2 1, −3
3 5 coins
4 Three tenths
5 Yes
6 1 hr 45 mins
7 32 km
8 61
9 34p
10 60 cm

Task 7c

1 27
2 36
3 20 cm
4 50
5 35
6 24
7 1500
8 7
9 1 kg
10 26 socks

Task 7d

Some solutions are:

Task 8a

1   0.69
2   34
3   97 cm
4   1500 grams
5   10 notebooks
6   90 minutes
7   110 cm (1.1 m)
8   6 days
9   3
10 52 weeks

Task 8b

[7]
[6 5 4 3 2 1]

[6 1]   [7 5 4 3 2]
[5 2]   [7 6 4 3 1]
[4 3]   [7 6 5 2 1]

[4 2 1]   [7 6 5 3]

Task 8c

1   5 boxes
2   90
3   10 cm
4   3, 7, 11, 18
5   9 hundredths
6   12 edges
7   14 (7 pairs)
8   100 children
9   180°
10 Triangular prism

Task 8d

1   900
2   36
3   32
4   49
5   85
6   39
7   15 minutes
8   24
9   9 coins
10 150 cm

Task 9a

a.

Glasgow	09:00	09:40
Falkirk	09:15	09:55
Linlithgow	09:25	10:05
Edinburgh	09:55	10:35

b. 30 minutes

c.

Edinburgh	10:10	10:50
Linlithgow	10:40	11:20
Falkirk	10:50	11:30
Glasgow	11:05	11:45

Task 9b

11 cubes
3 cubes
6 cubes

Task 9c

1   10 buns
2   10 metres
3   5 coins
4   750 grams
5   40 cm
6   200 ml
7   3 right angles
8   500
9   Quadrilateral
10 1, 3, 5, 15

Task 9d

1   30
2   32
3   56
4   30
5   1.2
6   64
7   3
8   No
9   7 tenths (0.7)
10 750

Task 10a

1   31
2   26
3   54
4   2.5
5   5
6   200
7   8.5 or $8^1/2$
8   Three tenths
9   0.9
10 7

Task 10b

1   Yes
2   0.03
3   50p
4   90 mins (1.5 h)
5   1 hr 35 mins
6   April 2nd
7   20 cm
8   4 boxes
9   4:10 p.m.
10 Eight

Task 10c

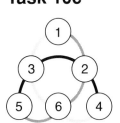

Task 10d

1   3 quarters ($^3/4$)
2   8
3   47
4   25
5   10.5 or $10^1/2$
6   21
7   60
8   Two fifths ($^2/5$)
9   22
10 5

Task 11a

1   15 minutes
2   3 boxes
3   Sphere
4   5
5   6 times
6   0, −5
7   4 m²
8   £2
9   20p
10 8 triangles

Task 11b

1   24
2   7
3   $3^1/4$ (3.25)
4   6
5   75
6   1.5 litres
7   33
8   81
9   1000
10 100

Task 11c

1   8
2   32
3   36
4   58
5   9
6   11
7   10
8   $1^1/4$ (1.25)
9   22
10 37

Task 11d

6	4	2
5		7
1	8	3

3	4	8
5		1
7	2	6

Task 12a

a. 1 hr 45 mins

b. 50 minutes

c. 25 minutes

d. 50 minutes

Task 12b

a. 8 cubes

b. 12 cubes

c. 6 cubes

d. 1 cube

Task 12c

1. 120°
2. 17 halves
3. 45p
4. £20
5. 91 days
6. 5 faces
7. 6 cm
8. 5 packets
9. 7:50 (10 to 8)
10. £1.07

Task 12d

1. 48
2. 34
3. 0.5 or $^1/_2$
4. 7
5. 34
6. 6
7. 9.5 or $9^1/_2$
8. 21
9. 4.2 or $4^1/_5$
10. 12

Task 13a

1. 60p
2. £2.40
3. £1.20
4. 70p
5. Putting
6. 40p
7. To skate
8. £1.20
9. £7.70
10. £1.80

Task 13b

1. 34
2. 100
3. 44
4. 1.5 or $1^1/_2$
5. 20
6. 100
7. 8
8. 0.75 kg
9. 75
10. 7

Task 13c

+	4	8	3	5	6
4	8	12	7	9	10
2	6	10	5	7	8
5	9	13	8	10	11
3	7	11	6	8	9

Task 13d

1. One sixth
2. 0
3. 55
4. 62
5. 500
6. 7 coins
7. 32
8. 1000 metres
9. 51
10. 2

Task 14a

1. 30
2. 33
3. 18
4. 90
5. 68
6. 200
7. 300
8. 4
9. 5
10. 6 cm

Task 14b

1. 5:25 (25 past 5)
2. 12
3. 5p
4. 2, 5, 12, 19
5. 45
6. 60p
7. 84
8. 4
9. 28 quarters
10. 6 cm

Task 14c

M A G I C
7 5 3 1 4

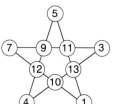

Task 14d

1. 62
2. 44
3. 55
4. 12
5. 7
6. 30
7. 12
8. 86
9. 30
10. 10.25 or $10^1/_4$

Task 15a

1. 30
2. 3.5 or $3^1/_2$
3. 0.75
4. 39
5. 10
6. 55
7. 46
8. 14
9. 24
10. 0.7 litres

Task 15b

1. 3 km
2. £20
3. 96
4. 450
5. 6
6. 2°C
7. 2nd August
8. 1.36 m
9. 90 seconds
10. 10 coins

Task 15c

1. 42
2. 7
3. 1000
4. One eighth ($^1/_8$)
5. 30
6. 1
7. 53
8. 22
9. 900
10. 88

Task 15d

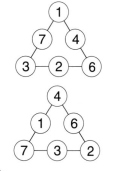

Answers: *Mental maths 4*

Mental Maths 4 introduces addition and subtraction of pairs of two-digit numbers and the addition of a series of single digits. Tables to 10×10, and small multiples of 11 or 12, are covered. Multiplication and division of whole numbers by 10 or 100 is consolidated and extended to 1000. Simple fractions and percentages are included, with estimates of measurements, simple conversions of one metric unit to another and calculations of areas, volumes and perimeters. Terms like square, cube, multiple, and factor, types of angles, and some imperial measures in common use, are used.

Task 1a
1. 74
2. 42
3. 15
4. 70
5. 70
6. 3.21 metres
7. 4.5 or $4^1/2$
8. 11
9. 16
10. 400

Task 1b
1. 33
2. 40 litres
3. 2017
4. 15p
5. 33 people
6. 49
7. 60p
8. 44
9. 13p
10. 18 triangles

Task 1c
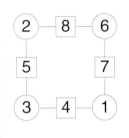

Task 1d
1. 28
2. 2.5 or $2^1/2$
3. 58
4. 49
5. 93
6. 758 pence
7. 50
8. 20
9. 63
10. 30

Task 2a
1. 4 full crates
2. 60p
3. 480 km
4. 3 kg
5. 6
6. 162
7. 0.27, 0.9, 1.3
8. 100 cm²
9. 320
10. 5 boxes

Task 2b
1. 49
2. 96
3. 37
4. 8.5 or $8^1/2$
5. 64
6. 72
7. 15 coins
8. 7
9. 57
10. 23

Task 2c
1. 56
2. 12
3. 8
4. 46
5. 36
6. 50
7. 18
8. 5.25 or $5^1/4$
9. 15 coins
10. 56 days

Task 2d
Greatest value is 33p. One solution is this.

5p	4p	2p
4p	1p	5p
3p	5p	4p

Task 3a
1. 9
2. 60p
3. 30th March
4. 80
5. 24 cm²
6. 180
7. 18:20 hours
8. 16p
9. 11 days
10. 60p

Task 3b

20p
35p
40p
55p
70p
75p
90p
£1.10

Task 3c
1. 90° (270°)
2. 2 metres
3. 36
4. 400
5. 4
6. £120
7. 6 litres
8. 300
9. 0.75 kg
10. 4 cm²

Task 3d
1. 56
2. 16
3. 22
4. 8.25 or $8^1/4$
5. 11
6. 81
7. 600
8. 37
9. 9
10. 3150

Task 4a
1. 116
2. 9
3. 90p
4. 91
5. 7.25 or $7^1/4$
6. 5000
7. 37
8. 40
9. 13
10. 8

Task 4b
Greatest total:
$9 + 7 + 6 + 8 = 30$
Smallest total:
$1 + 3 + 7 + 3 = 14$

With diagonal links
Greatest total:
$8 + 7 + 9 + 8 = 32$
Smallest total:
$5 + 3 + 3 + 4 = 15$

Task 4c
1. 6
2. 72
3. 32
4. 47
5. 7400
6. 45
7. 1 000 000
8. 19
9. 0
10. One eighth ($^1/8$)

Task 4d
1. 48
2. in
3. is
4. 65
5. as
6. 56
7. 8
8. 40
9. 24
10. 400

Task 5a
1. 110
2. 6500
3. 38
4. 12
5. 75
6. 26
7. 4
8. 18
9. 9
10. 18

Task 5b
1. 17p
2. 10 metres
3. A kite
4. Six eighths
5. 6
6. 9
7. £54
8. 200 ml
9. 600
10. 120°

Task 5c
a.

20	1	12
3	11	19
10	21	2

b.

1	15	14	4
12	6	7	9
8	10	11	5
13	3	2	16

Task 5d
1. 59
2. 4
3. 4000
4. 29
5. 71
6. 81
7. 16
8. 24
9. 21
10. 7

Task 6a
1. 39p
2. 7 days
3. 30 metres
4. £1.28
5. 43 210
6. Tuesday
7. 10027
8. 1.4 metres
9. 7
10. 25%

Task 6b
1. 81
2. 63
3. 8
4. 100
5. 24
6. 18
7. 12
8. £3.50
9. −1
10. 44

Task 6c
Two solutions are:

1	6	7
8	9	4
3	2	5

1	2	3
8	9	4
7	6	5

Task 6d
1. 71
2. 20
3. 23
4. 216
5. 10
6. 29
7. 0.7 litres
8. 44
9. 11
10. 550 pence.

Task 7a
1. 100
2. 68
3. 27
4. 19
5. 71
6. Five tenths
7. 143 cm
8. 40
9. 22
10. 84

Task 7b
1. 90p
2. 208
3. 3 boxes
4. 1.6, 0.61, 0.16
5. 24 cm³
6. 8 km
7. 470 (or 475)
8. 60°
9. 70%
10. 11 triangles

Task 7c
1. 34
2. 508
3. 14
4. 26
5. 75
6. 6
7. 595
8. 1560 mm
9. 42
10. 15 quarters

Task 7d

A	B	C	D	E	F
4	8	9	1	3	6

a. $E + F = C$
b. $F + B = DA$
c. $E \times F = DB$
d. $F \times B = AB$

Task 8a
1. 35 cm²
2. 3 004 007
3. 54 marbles
4. 63 days
5. A trapezium
6. Two sixths
7. 25 cm²
8. 400
9. 24
10. 45p

Task 8b

Put 26 kg in each suitcase.

18 kg and 8 kg in one suitcase.

3 kg, 14 kg, 7 kg and 2 kg in the other suitcase.

Task 8c
1. 30°
2. 100
3. 44p
4. 50%
5. 45 seconds
6. 103 060
7. 15 °C
8. 5 crates
9. 25 cm
10. 6 paths

Task 8d
1. 27
2. 3
3. 8
4. 48
5. 84
6. 100
7. 5500 ml
8. 27
9. 300
10. 3 hundredths

Task 9a
1. 37p
2. 66p
3. 48p
4. 35p
5. 20p
6. 58p
7. £1.80
8. £2.20
9. 18p
10. £3.30

Task 9b
a.
```
   46
 + 28
 ────
   74
```
b.
```
   38
 − 29
 ────
    9
```
c.
```
   33
 + 87
 ────
  120
```

Task 9c
1. 30 cm
2. 42 millimetres
3. 40%
4. 9
5. 7
6. 20 pens
7. £2.74
8. 13
9. 1 500 000
10. 75 bottles

Task 9d
1. 246
2. 16
3. 64
4. 34
5. 29
6. 85
7. 3600 metres
8. 496
9. 4050
10. No

Task 10a
1. 3.4 or 3²/₅
2. 43
3. £0.60 or 60p
4. 83
5. 39
6. 6068
7. 50
8. 1800 grams
9. One eighth
10. 3 thousandths

Task 10b
1. £4.07
2. 1.1 metres
3. Four sixths
4. 36, 43
5. Parallelogram
6. No
7. 23
8. 1936
9. 8 boxes
10. 11 cm² or 12 cm²

Task 10c

```
      5   4

          3
    ×
  ──────────
  1   6   2
```

Task 10d
1. 91
2. 56
3. 4.2 or 4¹/₅
4. 27
5. 50
6. 241
7. 300 cm
8. 5903
9. 65
10. 300 (or 270)

Task 11a
1. 120°
2. 5
3. 35 miles
4. 1.6 metres
5. 1000
6. £5000
7. 12 ribbons
8. £1.32
9. 6 km
10. A sphere

Task 11b
1. 27
2. 51
3. 5.4 or 5²/₅
4. 13
5. 0.65 litres
6. 20 millimetres
7. 0.125
8. 112
9. 3 dozen
10. 207

Task 11c
1. 72
2. 76
3. 10000
4. 69
5. 6.6 or 6³/₅
6. 126
7. 0.85 kg
8. 26
9. 2
10. 2500

Task 11d

Total	200	50
Red	28	7
Yellow	56	14
Pink	44	11
Purple	52	13
White	20	5

Task 12a

1   A and D (27)

2   A and E (9)

3   B and C (32)

4   B and E (81)

5   A and C (0.7)

Task 12b

×	4	8	3	5	6
7	28	56	21	35	42
2	8	16	6	10	12
5	20	40	15	25	30
9	36	72	27	45	54

Task 12c

1   13 °C
2   288
3   75p
4   32, 76, 130
5   1 (or 1.0)
6   a. 140 b. 235
7   £9.06
8   0.375
9   Cylinder
10 30

Task 12d

1   236
2   110
3   18
4   32
5   23
6   141
7   3 (or 3.0)
8   9
9   1800
10 1, 2, 3, 4, 6, 12

Task 13a

1   33 and 17
2   25 and 13
3   17 and 18
4   18 and 33
5   34 (d17)
6   13 and 28
7   a. 48 b. 86
8   28
9   d13 and d17
10 17 and 33

Task 13b

1   1990
2   46
3   54
4   136
5   32
6   7
7   26
8   0.025 litres
9   42
10 6400

Task 13c

¹1	6	²1
³1	2	1
5	⁴2	7

Task 13d

1   8.4
2   143
3   4007
4   126
5   52
6   75 coins
7   67
8   0.036 kg
9   33
10 48 months

Task 14a

1   153
2   54
3   16
4   23
5   15
6   425
7   10.8 or 10⁴/5
8   0.075 km
9   One eighth ($^1/8$)
10 99

Task 14b

1   £2.73
2   8 ounces
3   £10
4   Cone
5   4.3
6   0.45 metres
7   70
8   2000
9   304
10 a. 700 b. 350

Task 14c

For example,

$$
\begin{array}{ccc}
182 & 236 & 519 \\
\underline{493} & \underline{745} & \underline{327} \\
675 & 981 & 846 \\
\end{array}
$$

Other solutions are
possible.

Task 14d

1   41
2   15
3   24
4   Yes
5   144
6   Four eighths
7   77
8   0.085 metres
9   49
10 60

Task 15a

1   26
2   9.8 or 9⁴/5
3   36
4   10000
5   143
6   16 ounces
7   9
8   0.1 kg
9   20
10 No

Task 15b

1   210°
2   20p (£0.20)
3   1000 miles
4   180
5   6 ways
6   8p
7   57, 59, 61
8   207015
9   21
10 6 and 6

Task 15c

1   125
2   35
3   36
4   183
5   400
6   34
7   0.05 km
8   16
9   2100
10 8 pints

Task 15d

T R I C K
12 14 11 8 10

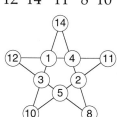